"*Called to Parish Ministry: Identity, Challenges, and Spirituality of Lay Ministers* by two dedicated professionals is an outstanding contribution to the growing number of ministry books. Greg Dues and Barbara Walkley offer sound theory and inspiring ideas from a background of study rooted in sacred scripture and church tradition, skillfully tempered by their personal experience of ministry.

"*Called to Parish Ministry* presents parish ministry as the treasure still partially hidden in the field even after 2000 years. It awaits the committed use of the gifts and skills of qualified lay ministers who can unearth the full value of such ministry for the kingdom.

"It can meet a real need in college classes dealing with the theology and practice of parish ministry."

Amata Fabbro, O.P.
Aquinas College, Grand Rapids, Michigan

"Most of this book is filled with clusters of very practical hints on how to minister in the Catholic church. Delightfully written, it should be required reading for all who minister to Catholics today who are struggling to live the Christian life in this global village."

Frances Kelly Sheets, O.S.C., Ph.D.
Planning & Management Information Systems

"Dues and Walkley present a vision of parish ministry that is both down-to-earth and inspiring. Their words challenge parish ministers to be first and foremost authentic human beings. In times when the unity of our church is often threatened by factional disputes among its ministers, this book is a godsend. It probes beneath our controversies to the basics of ministry: call, enthusiasm, creativity, mission, and community. For the good of our church, I hope this book gets used!"

Rev. Tom Krieg
Onlaska, Wisconsin

"The 'explosion of ministry' of which this book speaks can evoke feelings of excitement, anxiety, or confusion, depending on one's standpoint. Dues and Walkley provide an excellent guide to interpreting the phenomenon in a way that is both faithful to the tradition and open to what the Spirit may be saying to the churches in our day. All in all, an excellent guide to 'the maze of ministry' in our day."

Rev. John Joe Spring
All Hallows Mission
and Ministry Institute, Dublin

"I found this book hopeful and visionary. It is written in a direct, practical style while addressing with depth the issues facing lay ministers. Rooted in a collaborative and communal model of parish ministry, it provides a thorough exploration of what Catholic ministry requires in our pluralistic, contemporary parishes. It also provides a multi-faceted approach for the spirituality of lay ministers. I highly recommend it!"

Barbara J. Fleischer, Ph.D.
Loyola Institute for Ministry

"Books about ministry are easy to find these days. But in *Called to Parish Ministry* the authors have provided us with an eminently readable, warmly supportive resource for and about parish ministers. Anyone involved in parish ministry today will find its insights clarifying and helpful."

Marliss Rogers
Co-author, *New Practical Guide for Parish Councils*
Editor, *Weekly Prayer Services for Parish Meetings*

"With this book, we are finally one whole step closer to getting our eyes fixed on the needs of the parish, and not a day too soon from where I sit. Our parishes are crying for quality ministers. And increasingly they are finding them in people like Barbara Walkley and Greg Dues.

"Read this book. Think of it as a report from the front lines, a hope-filled survival manual from two who know."

Rev. Jeffrey J. Donner, Pastor

"This book will be of great help to any diocese, institute, or college engaged in the formation of ministers. Those serving as ministers will find insights and checkpoints that they will be able to affirm from personal experience. The book is well organized, well written, and easily read. There are excellent questions at the conclusion of every chapter that stimulate and engage the reader in dialogue with the authors and with one's own experience."

Sr. Lisa Marie Lazio, O.P.
Councilor of Life Development

# CALLED TO
# PARISH
# MINISTRY

### IDENTITY, CHALLENGES,
### AND SPIRITUALITY
### OF LAY MINISTERS

GREG DUES & BARBARA WALKLEY

TWENTY-THIRD PUBLICATIONS
THE COLUMBA PRESS

Published simultaneously by

Twenty-Third Publications
185 Willow Street
P.O. Box 180
Mystic, CT 06355
(203) 536-2611
800-321-0411

ISBN 0-89622-649-2
Library of Congress Catalog Card Number 94-62158

The Columba Press
93 The Rise
Mount Merrion, Blackrock
Co. Dublin
ISBN 1-85607-139-1

Printed in the U.S.A.

# Contents

# PART TWO:
## Taking an Honest Look at Our Identity

# PART THREE:
## Responding Maturely to Challenges

## PART FOUR:
## Paying Attention to Our Spirituality

# Introduction

Catholic parishes are alive and healthy. Large crowds gather for parish liturgies, worshiping with a fair amount of enthusiasm. Women and men serve in the sanctuary as lectors and ministers of Eucharist. Song leaders, choirs, and musicians help people raise their prayers and songs to God. Cheerful greeters, some of them children and teens, greet parishioners and visitors at the church doors. Women and men provide community hospitality with coffee, punch, and donuts after Masses.

Parishioners visit the homebound and patients in hospitals. Evangelization efforts, such as the adult catechumenate and welcome-back efforts, are taking hold. Renewal movements awaken new interest in Scripture and in community-building in small groups. New parish structures are in place and working: parish councils, commissions, and ad hoc committees.

Parishioners hear the gospel and respond, sometimes with great personal sacrifice, with efforts toward peace, justice, and human rights. Coordinated Christian service efforts reach out to the poor, the hungry, the homeless, the handicapped, the lonely, and the broken.

Schools consolidate to meet challenges of today more efficiently. Parish religious formation sessions are available for all ages. Catechists share the Word with creative techniques. Lay eucharistic ministers share the parish's holy bread with the sick and homebound. Parishioners sign up for comprehensive ministry training, preparing to take their place on pastoral teams. Women and men pursue undergraduate and graduate degrees to prepare for full-time ministry.

These and many more creative ministry opportunities flourish in Catholic parishes today. Because an increasing number of parishes are committed to team ministry, these ministries evolve and find direction within the context of the parish community rather than as individual efforts. The people in charge in contemporary parishes, whose names usually appear in the parish bulletins, coordinate these manifold efforts to bring about the reign of God in their part of the world. Depending on size of parish, they include the pastor, pastoral associates, principal, director of religious education, youth minister, catechumenate (RCIA) director, liturgist, and coordinator of outreach. Many of these team members have graduate degrees or at least years of special formation.

All of this takes place in parishes where yesterday saw only a team of priests and at most a parochial school faculty. This explosion of ministries involves mostly women and men who are not ordained. In fact, *lay* ministry is the exciting news of our times. It is still new enough that all the bugs have not been worked out. It is still new enough for lay ministers to wonder, "Who am I?" "What is my relation to the parish team?" "To the other parishioners?" It is also new enough to look for a spirituality that will support these new challenges and responsibilities.

*Called to Parish Ministry* is a support tool for non-ordained ministers in our Catholic parishes and addresses issues of special concern to them. The fact that this volume is concerned with only "lay" ministry should not be taken to mean that ministry should be divided into categories of lay and ordained. While ministries might be divided between church ministries and marketplace, sometimes called kingdom ministries, all ministry of whatever kind is ministry to and within God's reign. Our emphasis, however, is on *parish* ministry, and specifically on the needs of those women and men who are designated and/or commissioned for special service within the parish or other church-related institutions.

Our text, therefore, is intended for those who are clearly identified as ministers within the parish, whether volunteers or recipients of stipend or salary. This roll call of ministers includes those mentioned just above, as well as other ministers who have been on the scene since the late 1960s: pastoral ministers; pastoral associates, pastoral administrators, DREs, CREs, MREs, and liturgical musicians; school personnel, too, should be identified as ministers if their primary assignment and effort is to promote the reign of God. Other persons who would benefit from our text are those who serve in important leadership roles on councils and commissions and are seriously involved in that work.

In Part One we look at the big picture of ministry. We find in Christian Scriptures the seed of all ministry yesterday and today

(Chapter 1), and note that fundamentally all ministry is for the sake of the reign of God, which is not totally identified with the church community (2). Then we survey the history of ministry (3), showing how original forms of ministry consolidated and became associated with male celibates. It is obvious that dynamic shifts in our own times and new needs within the Catholic parishes call for renewal of parish ministries and the creative development of new ones as we come to grips with specific challenges, such as the role of women (4, 5, 6).

In Part Two we take an honest look at our identity, finding that our ministry has to happen in the context of a human church (7), a contemporary Catholic church (8), and a pluralistic church (9). Some of us are called to a ministry of leadership. Even if we are not, much of today's parish ministry is coordinated by or is accountable to leadership groups. This ministry of leadership is charting new courses today (10). We also have to come to grips with our functioning religious identity, in contrast to a theoretical identity and explain some obstacles we meet (11).

Lay ministry today faces a host of challenges. We examine these in Part Three. First of all, we need to develop a sense of confidence and find in ourselves, and in the Spirit who inflames us, a primary source of this confidence (12). Other sources of effective ministry—essential tools—are the powers of imagination and creativity (13). Taking our place in organized ministry brings along with it new insights into our own gifts and those of people with whom we share ministry (14). The day of the "lone ranger" has passed. We are called to minister effectively with others, facing with them the hurdles that come with joint efforts (15), including clashes in theologies (16), staying always open to change (17).

Effective human gifts and skills cannot substitute for a firmly rooted spirituality that will provide a solid foundation for our ministry. In Part Four we find our spiritual models in the pages of Scripture, challenged by a surprising God, who is sometimes different than we expected (18). If we want to be holy, contented, and effective ministers, we need to develop wholistic, healthy patterns (19). Sound spirituality and Christlike ministry depend upon commitment to key gospel qualities: simplicity (20), genuineness (21), a sense of service (22), and a healing touch (23). We find these qualities in the Christian Scriptures and especially in reflecting on the meaning and nature of ministry and discipleship.

Church ministries have not been finalized as we approach the third millennium. Lay ministers are challenged to tap into God's dream as part of their spirituality and find their personal dreams and dreams for the communities we serve (24).

Each chapter provides opportunity for reflection. These reflections are designed to challenge readers to come to grips in a practical way with their own ministry. These might also be used for group discussion as the participants share their hopes and thoughts about their ministry.

The environment for this book is ministry in the Western, or Latin, Roman Catholic church. Even within this environment, we realize, different forms and emphases of ministry exist throughout the world—and throughout North America. Even neighboring parishes can have radically different insights into what the mystery of church is and should be. Obviously, lay ministry will take different forms in different parishes. It may not even exist in some.

*Called to Parish Ministry*, therefore, does not pretend to meet every situation or to represent every theological conviction. Our intent is to provide a popular and practical overview of lay ministry and issues that relate to it, rather than a detailed analysis. For purposes of simplicity, extensive documentation in footnotes has been avoided. Instead, generous quotes from Scripture and current theological literature are included in the text. We hope these will promote reflection and further discussion. A selected reading list is included at the end of the book.

Final word on any of these issues is not intended. More can be said, and will be said, as our Catholic church continues to come to grips with these issues.

In writing this book we have drawn on decades of a variety of parish, diocesan, and special ministry experiences, several graduate programs, and the continuing formation derived from our experiences and reading. We write at a time when tensions continue within the Catholic church regarding such matters as the role of women, effects of priest shortage, the nature of parish ministries, and inclusive language. We feel that these tensions, like those in the past, provide us with insights into the mystery of our own historical moment.

*Called to Parish Ministry* is intended for lay ministers' private use and reflection and for discussion with others. It will also serve as a practical tool in diocesan ministry formation programs, college courses, and orientation sessions for pastoral teams and leadership groups.

# PART ONE

# Overview
# of Ministry

# — 1 —

# The Beginning
# of Ministry

## Excitement of New Times

We walk through narrow streets of the large cosmopolitan, Greek-speaking city of Antioch, capital of Syria, the third largest city in our Roman Empire. Scattered around the city are small pockets of Jews committed to a new way of living and believing. This "new way" was preached for the first time by Jesus of Nazareth in neighboring Palestine just a few years earlier. We found similar communities last month while visiting Jerusalem in the land of Jesus.

Nothing in particular distinguishes the families in Antioch from their Jewish neighbors. On Sabbath mornings you will find them in their synagogues as before. Many of them were Gentile converts to Judaism before committing themselves to the way of Jesus. They listen to the Hebrew Scriptures with a cooperative attitude and raise their voices in heartfelt prayer. Sometimes, however, an argument breaks out during discussion—about Jesus of Nazareth. Followers of his new way become ecstatic testifying to his words and deeds. They are convinced that a new day has dawned. They declare emphatically that these are new times because the reign of God is now among them. They insist that the powerful presence of God became evident in the words and deeds of Jesus. At times they refer to Jesus as the Christ. The anointed one. The chosen one. The Messiah. The Lord!

We are curious about these people who seem so excited and who have such dynamic convictions. Do they meet outside the synagogue? "Yes," they tell us, "every Sabbath night, the eve of the first day of the week." Probing further, we discover that there is no one place reserved for these weekly assemblies. Nothing like a synagogue. They meet in their own neighborhoods, in one of their homes, usually the same one every week over a period of time.

Do they have someone in charge? A rabbi? "We are like the sheep Jesus talked about. We have to have shepherds, so we have teachers and prophets, just as we do in our synagogues."

Then we hear comforting words of hospitality and service. "Do you need anything? A place to stay? Some food? Would you like to meet with us tonight in Aquila's home? Would you like to hear more about Jesus?"

These synagogues were local Jewish assembly halls for the reading of Hebrew Scriptures, especially the Torah, for prayer and instruction. They were vital centers of community life that had become popular during the Babylonian exile (587-537 B.C.E.) to keep faith alive when contact with the temple in Jerusalem was impossible. At the time of Jesus, the synagogues were modeled after free associations in the Graeco-Roman culture. Every village and the neighborhoods of large cities in Palestine had a synagogue. So did the cities throughout the Jewish Diaspora, settlements of Jews in other lands where the Jewish population was much larger than in Palestine. Most synagogues outside of Palestine functioned within the prevailing Greek culture. They attracted large numbers of Gentiles as members. Other people, called the God-fearers, did not become members but maintained a close relationship with the synagogues. This synagogue system throughout the Diaspora became a key factor in the rapid spread of Christianity.

Hellenist followers of Jesus—Jews who had adopted the Greek culture—had fled to Antioch from Jerusalem during the persecution that followed the stoning of Stephen. It was in Antioch that followers of Jesus were first called Christians (Acts 11:26). There they continued to preach the way of Jesus. At first they were considered simply as a sect, one of many that occasionally flared up in synagogues. Then came an uneasy alliance followed by schism as followers of the new way broke from the synagogue in all the major population centers of the Middle East. Actually, instead of breaking union with the synagogues, in many places Christians were expelled for what were considered heretical beliefs, blasphemies. How dare they call Jesus Lord! How dare they welcome uncircumcised Gentiles to their tables!

Even separated from the synagogues, followers of Jesus in Antioch displayed a strong pluralism and conflict within their own communities of faith. Believers were on a continuum from extreme right (circumcision and all Jewish traditions must be observed) to extreme left (believers are free from all Jewish traditions). This pluralism, more complicated than a simple division between Jews and Gentiles, was characteristic of other major centers of Judaism, such as Jerusalem.

The Christian communities at Antioch knew Paul and Barnabas as resident missionaries. Eventually, those Christians who claimed more freedom from Jewish traditions sent these two to represent their liberal—even radical—cause before leaders in the mother church at Jerusalem (Acts 15:1ff). Although there seemed to have been a positive hearing on this issue, Antioch later became the scene of an argument between Peter and Paul over this same question concerning Gentile believers: How much of the Jewish tradition were they bound to observe (Galatians 2:12)? It seems that Paul's view lost out and he left Antioch soon after this for other missionary efforts. For a while, Peter stayed on and provided a moderating influence. In time, this church would become predominantly Gentile. It was most probably here in Antioch about 85 C.E. that Matthew wrote his gospel.

This historical aside about religious conflict among the early followers of Jesus is important for contemporary Catholics tempted to be scandalized at current conflicts. (See Chapter 9, Ministering in a Pluralistic Church.)

Antioch continued to be an important Christian center. At the turn of the first century, Antioch Christians chose the gifted Ignatius (d. 107) as their bishop. He was the first to use the term "catholic" to describe the church. He wrote six letters on his way to martyrdom in Rome. In them he promoted a strong three-tiered structure of community leadership: one bishop, a council of presbyters, or elders, and a group of deacons. The local bishop was head of the assembly and chief teacher.

In its new situation separated from Judaism, a Christian church becoming more and more Gentile, forms of ministry and structures of the local community evolved in new directions. But they evolved from key ministries inherited from Jewish synagogues: *elders*—

always a group—with authority to coordinate and oversee the community's religious and social activities and to preside over assemblies; *teachers* who handed down in their particular communities an evolving religious tradition that reflected the influence of certain apostles, such as Peter and Paul, and of differing religious emphases (Jewish Christians or Gentile Christians); and *prophets* who were gifted to stir up enthusiasm and to make God's word present and effective. Incidentally, the function of elder, or presbyter, was originally borrowed from civic functionaries in the Graeco-Roman culture.

We have journeyed far from those early Christian centers. During twenty centuries our Catholic faith has touched virtually every people on planet Earth. In turn, these people have touched our Catholic faith. Beginning already in apostolic times, people's cultures and social structures radically influenced and changed Christianity's patterns of ministry. Primitive communities of believers had someone in charge who was responsible for leading and coordinating the pastoral efforts of the community: "But we appeal to you, brothers and sisters, to respect those who labor among you and have charge of you in the Lord and admonish you; esteem them highly in love because of their work" (1 Thessalonians 5:12–13).

Someone, usually a leader of the community, such as a teacher, prophet, or head of a house church, naturally led them in remembering the words and deeds of Jesus and in the blessing and sharing of the eucharistic bread and cup. They designated others, male and female, to look after the emergency needs of co-believers. Many of these early believers were slaves with personal needs similar to repressed peoples today. Other services similar to our unemployment benefits were needed because of fluctuations in the economy, just as today.

These forms of ministry were not the same in all the Christian centers. Already in those early days, different religious experiences engendered different kinds of communities and ministries. Communities associated with Paul seemed to have been more free and charismatic—and Gentile—than those founded by the Twelve. Community leadership in Pauline churches rested mostly with teachers and prophets. Other churches depended more on the leadership exercised by elders, who often assumed the ministry similar to that exercised by teachers and prophets in Pauline communities. Different cultures in the Roman empire also gave different nuances to local leadership and ministries. Jerusalem in Palestine was not identical with Antioch in Syria or Alexandria in Egypt. Corinth was different still. So was Rome.

While ministry—like the gospel that defines it and gives it life—was firmly established from the beginning, our careful distinctions of modern times would have confused the early Christians and their leaders. They were very pragmatic. Their words for ministry describe responses to needs in their communities of faith and neighborhoods: teaching, preaching, prophesying, serving, reconciling, healing, leading, and overseeing.

These Christians responded to obvious needs with enthusiasm, but were not at all preoccupied, as we are today, with fine and even legal distinction of roles, titles, and jurisdictions. They would not understand our preoccupation with *ordained* and *lay* ministers. Yet they would always know who was in charge and who held the purse to share community funds with the needy. If you wanted to hear more about the words and deeds of Jesus, teachers were available. During their weekly assembly, a prophet or two could be counted on for an encouraging message: "The prophet . . . speaks to people for their upbuilding, their encouragement, their consolation" (1 Corinthians 14:3).

These teachers and prophets also presided over the Eucharist in many communities. If another community, close by or far away, needed a first hearing of the gospel, the local community would send an apostle or evangelist. Are you sick? There were healers. Are you depressed and frightened? There were consolers.

Even though ministry evolved into new forms over the centuries, we need to reflect upon these "beginning times" to appreciate the fundamentals of ministry. The gospels, the Acts of the Apostles, and letters to the churches offer abundant information about these fundamentals. We are used to our own forms today where priestly ministry flows from the sacrament of orders and lay ministry from contracts or commissioning ceremonies. These are only contemporary human ways of identifying and coordinating what really flows as lavish gifts from the Spirit of God to Christian communities. Admittedly, authors and editors of the Christian Scriptures recorded an idealized version of how these early Christian communities functioned. Luke wrote the Acts of the Apostles, for example, a generation after the events described, to promote a sense of single-mindedness among these early Christians. Today we would say that he wanted to put a better "spin" on the events. As we saw above, the Christian community in Antioch had a lengthy history of internal conflict, with groups rallying around different apostles and different theologies. (See Chapter 7, Ministering in a Human Church, and Chapter 9, Ministering in a Pluralistic Church.)

What is so striking in earliest Scriptures, especially in the Pauline letters, is a rich variety of gifts or ministries evident in first-century Christian communities:

> Now there are varieties of gifts, but the same Spirit; and there are varieties of services, but the same Lord; and there are varieties of activities, but it is the same God who activates all of them in everyone. To each is given the manifestation of the Spirit for the common good. To one is given through the Spirit the utterance of wisdom, and to another the utterance of knowledge according to the same Spirit, to another faith by the same Spirit, to another gifts of healing by the same Spirit, to another the working of miracles, to another prophecy, to another the discernment of spirits, to another various kinds of tongues, to another the interpretation of tongues. All these are activated by one and the same Spirit, who allots to each one individually just as the Spirit chooses (1 Corinthians 12:4–11).

> We have gifts that differ according to the grace given to us: prophecy, in proportion to faith; ministry, in ministering; the teacher, in teaching; the exhorter, in exhortation; the giver, in generosity; the leader, in diligence; the compassionate, in cheerfulness (Romans 12:6–8).

> The gifts he gave were that some would be apostles, some prophets, some evangelists, some pastors and teachers, to equip the saints for the work of ministry for the building up of the body of Christ, until all of us come to unity of the faith and of the knowledge of the Son of God, to maturity, to the measure of the full stature of Christ (Ephesians 4:11–13).

There is an obvious excitement associated with this variety of ministries in emerging Christian communities. It is not an exaggeration to say that these women and men were all charged up. They could not have testified to a developed theology under the guidance of the Holy Spirit, but they allowed themselves to be swept along by a new mood and excitement that we would associate with the Spirit. They were not in control of those new times. Paul had to set up guidelines eventually to coordinate this enthusiasm (1 Corinthians 14). These early Christians were not so far removed from a new Spirit's fire and winds of the Pentecost event when enthusiastic believers were accused of being drunk. Lay ministers today often experience a similar enthusiasm, or "high." This happens not only in ministry activity but also in Spirit-filled meetings, workshops, retreats, and other times when committed ministers assemble.

## Quick Turn in Ministry

Soon after these earliest times in Christianity, the rich variety of ministries began to melt away. By the turn of the first century, seventy years after the death and resurrection of Jesus, there is evident development of and preoccupation with leadership ministries in the communities. Neither Jesus nor the apostles had left a blueprint of church structure. Admission that the end times and a final coming of the Lord were not imminent forced Christian communities to pay more attention to the future and to their human structures. The death of the original Twelve, the threat of heresy from within Christian communities, especially Gnosticism which minimized the humanity of Jesus, and actual persecution from outside by Roman civil authorities also prompted leaders to solidify church structure. The more free and charismatic churches began to lose out to the process of institutionalization. House churches where only a dozen or so gathered evolved into Christian communities with need for larger and different kinds of assembly areas.

A more hierarchical leadership structure gradually replaced the collegial administrative coordination by a group of elders. Previously one elder often represented the group and would preside over the eucharistic assembly. Now a three-fold ranking of bishop (guardian/overseer), presbyter (elder), and deacon (minister) became popular. An *episkopos*, or bishop, chosen by the people from among the elders in the early years of Christianity, gradually assumed most of the ministry of teacher and prophet. Deacons became assistants to these bishops. Presbyters continued to exercise leadership in local communities in outlying areas.

As the second century unfolded, church leadership modeled itself more and more on the forms of civic authority in the Roman empire. Even though intermittent persecutions carried out by these same Roman officials continued to threaten Christians, the influence of culture was so strong that Christians felt no contradiction in imitating Roman forms in their Christian communities.

Good deeds continued to flourish in these communities. The need to hold communities together during a time of accelerated growth dictated an emphasis on a weekly eucharistic assembly and a ministry associated with it. At the same time, the need for tighter organization and control continued to increase. The free-form ministry and multiple charisms prominent during Paul's time faded away. Preoccupation with centralized authority replaced evangelization. By the third century the ministry of bishops, presbyters, and deacons had become almost totally invested in presiding over liturgical assemblies and exercising leadership. These official ministers were designated by a ritual of laying on of hands, or ordination. By the end of the third century this new order was in place and in major population centers these ministries had become the full-time *modus operandi*.

A further evolution occurred. These bishops came to be considered *priests*, and presbyters became the *assistant priests* of the New Covenant. This new notion of priesthood became popular because of two historical events. Organized Jewish temple worship with its priesthood faded from the scene when Roman armies destroyed Jerusalem in 70 C.E. Also, pagan temples with their priesthood began to lose favor in the Roman empire. Until then there was a general bias among Christians against assuming the role of priesthood because it was associated with the Jewish temple and with pagan temples. It was enough that they had the special priesthood of Jesus Christ earned through his death (letter to Hebrews) and a general symbolic priesthood of all the baptized because they were, in their new Scriptures echoing the Hebrew Scriptures, "a chosen race, a royal priesthood" (1 Peter 2:9).

While this transition to having a priesthood was taking place, it became popular to apply Jewish cultic terminology and images of sacrifice and priesthood from the Hebrew Scriptures to the eucharistic meal and community leadership. These images gradually replaced the more original gospel banquet images of the eucharist. Fixed stone and marble altars began to replace wooden, movable banquet tables.

By the mid-200s, bishops and they alone were considered priests who presided over the eucharist. Elders, or presbyters, served as substitutes when the bishop could not be present. As eucharistic communities multiplied, especially with legal freedom of religion beginning in 313 C.E., presbyters took on the role of priest in local communities, presiding at eucharist, exercising leadership, and maintaining a bond with the mother church and its bishop. The bishop continued to be the chief pastor of a region, called a *diocese* in Roman law.

This identification of ministry with the community's ordained leadership caused a division between laity and clergy (from *kleros*, "lot," or "inheritance," in the sense of the Levites in Hebrew Scriptures whose only inheritance came from the Lord [Numbers 18:20]). Ordination set clergy apart as sacred persons, marked for ritual ministry. The laity were *ministered to* instead of *ministering*. When Christianity became allied with the Roman empire and became the state religion in the fourth century, the clergy assumed many of the privileges and trappings of civil officials. In some places they were also called upon to perform civil acts.

This identification of ministry with the activities of ordained bishops, priests, and deacons became so ingrained in the thinking of these Christians that a ministry belonging by nature to the non-ordained disappeared from common thinking early in the history of Christianity.

## Questions for Reflection and Discussion

1. What features of ministry described in the Christian Scriptures would attract you?

2. Do you feel that ministry is more effective with a freestyle leadership or with a clearly defined leadership? Why?

3. Are you comfortable with the evolution of ministry into forms of priesthood? What was lost? What was gained?

# — 2 —

# "Thy Kingdom Come"

Let's stay with our Christian sisters and brothers of that fresh Christianity of New Testament times and reflect further upon their example, attitude, and convictions about ministry. What motivated them? How did their activity differ from that of their unbaptized friends, family, and neighbors? We can look to them for fresh insights even though we realize that those times cannot—and probably should not—be revived.

## Ministry and the Reign of God

Those early Christians were overwhelmed by a conviction that the reign of God had come—and was still coming more and more through their good deeds and evangelizing. The Greek word *basileia* is usually translated by "kingdom" or "reign." These words do not evoke the same effective images in our contemporary thinking as they did for them. It meant that God had been present and active as Jesus touched and healed the sick, forgave the sinner, consoled the grieving, fed the hungry, freed people from their demons, condemned injustice, and announced the arrival of "new times." The reign of God was the focus and motive of everything Jesus said and did. This powerful, saving, and loving presence of God in Christ continued now in their own activities. They acted in the powerful name of Jesus, believing that *Christ acted through them*. He continued, in their belief, to forge a new covenant between God and people through their ministry. They sensed a new climate or atmosphere permeating their communities as they submitted to this God and committed themselves to a renewed way of believing and living. They experienced God as powerfully present in their assemblies, in their evangelizing efforts among those who had not yet come to faith, in their healing of the sick in Christ's name, in their sharing of personal goods with the needy. Sometimes these Christians experienced this presence of God to the very depths of their beings! Pentecost was not an isolated event.

## Deliberate and Evident Ministry

These Christians were fully aware that the presence of God did not happen as they sat idly by. They knew that the reign of God was not complete yet; in fact, it was only just beginning. They knew this as they prayed "Thy kingdom come. . . ." These new times of God's powerful and saving presence would come only through their deliberate and public efforts. Ministry for them—and for us—goes far beyond a cheerful "Have a nice day!" Through their diligent efforts, the wonder of God's plan began to make all things new. Through their striving, a new age was beginning. Excited with new opportunities, these Christians took Jesus' counsel to heart:

> You are the light of the world. A city built on a hill cannot be hid. No one after lighting a lamp puts it under the bushel basket, but on the lamp stand, and it gives light to all in the house. In the same way, let your light shine before others, so that they may see your good works and give glory to your Father in heaven (Matthew 5:14–16).

They testified and evangelized openly, even at the risk of life itself. Stephen was probably more a typical example than an exception of these committed believers. In Acts 6:8ff he is described as "full of grace and power," doing "great wonders and signs among the people." Condemned for his ministry to the new way preached by Jesus, he continued testifying publicly until the stones of martyrdom silenced him.

## Comprehensive Ministry

Early Christian communities were pockets of faith within larger neighborhoods of those ancient villages and cities of later New

Testament times. Believers were very conscious of what it took to preserve their faith, celebrate it, and grow in it. At the risk of over-simplification, these communities were more akin to non-conforming ing communes than to our large Catholic parishes of today. Or to the structure and spirit of *communidades de base* (base communities) popular primarily in the Latin American countries and now emerging in the Catholic church in other continents.

The early church communities were also conscious of their social and physical needs. They applied themselves to whatever the local group needed:

> Now during those days, when the disciples were increasing in number, the Hellenists complained against the Hebrews because their widows were being neglected in the daily distribution of food. And the twelve called together the whole community of the disciples and said, "It is not right that we should neglect the word of God in order to wait on tables. Therefore, friends, select from among yourselves seven men of good standing, full of the Spirit and of wisdom, whom we may appoint to this task, while we, for our part, will devote ourselves to prayer and to serving the word." What they said pleased the whole community. . . (Acts 6:1ff).

Luke writes this almost a generation after the events, idealizing early Christianity's ministry response to specific needs. In this case, the need arose from tensions caused by pluralism of language and culture within the Christian communities and by conflicts about fidelity to or freedom from Jewish traditions. Basic ministries had to function, and function in a comprehensive way, even when the local church community was preoccupied with cultural and religious conflicts.

These early Christians had to be reminded often that the reign of God was not co-extensive with their local small groups gathered around simple tables in house churches. They were not free from the temptation to claim that salvation belonged to them alone. Segments of early Christian Scriptures were preserved to correct this attitude, such as Jesus' parables about the lost sheep, the lost coin, and the lost son. Even though they thought of themselves as the faithful ninety-nine sheep, ministry efforts had to be expended on the lost sheep, to all nations of the world. Even though they were faithful to God, they must not claim special favors for this when the lost came home. These local communities sent out missionaries, like Barnabas and Paul, to make evident the presence and power of God. "Thy kingdom come!" This comprehensive nature of ministry is emphasized at the conclusion of the gospel according to Matthew:

> And Jesus came and said to them, "All authority in heaven and earth has been given to me. Go therefore and make disciples of all nations, baptizing them in the name of the Father and of the Son and of the Holy Spirit and teaching them to obey everything that I have commanded you. And remember, I am with you always, to the end of the age" (28:18ff).

## Multi-Dimensional Ministry

What the early Christians recognized and experienced in God's activity and in Jesus' gospel of new times was new and unique. The reign of God was to be radically different from religion as they had known it. It was not a new religion. The entire public ministry of Jesus had been non-liturgical. While these disciples of Jesus continued to celebrate their religious traditions, often with new meaning, they came to their baptism with a kind of freedom from emphasis on religious externals. Something new was happening; the Spirit of God was blowing fresh through their communities.

Ministry, therefore, was not highly organized or liturgically oriented at the beginning. It is important to reflect upon the truth that the reign of God as the Christian Scriptures testify to it is not synonymous with the church as we know it. Otherwise, we might continue the prevalent errors of the past, namely, that ministry is limited to "a church thing."

Some ministry will always be oriented to the needs of a definable church community. We cannot erase the fact that contemporary Catholicism is a highly organized—centralized—religion with highly coordinated liturgical assemblies. Religion does need its priests. But the lavishness of God's grace spills out beyond liturgical assemblies. And this spilling still happens today as it did in those early generations—through the dedication, gifts, and efforts of women and men. Some of these are ordained, and some are officially designated and/or commissioned as lay ministers. However, the gospel call to service goes beyond this official ministry. It goes out to all the baptized faithful who feed the hungry, clothe the naked, shelter the homeless, visit the imprisoned, serve on housing boards and crime control commissions, coordinate soup kitchens, fill thanksgiving baskets, console the bereaved, give hope to the separated and divorced, and oppose violence of all kinds.

Baptized people who carry their faith and gospel convictions with them wherever they go and wherever they work and play have limitless opportunities to be instruments of God's wonderful grace and powerful reign.

Local church communities will always have a role in this broader ministry because it is within the parish that the faithful are nourished with an effective word and sacrament. It is within the parish that their enthusiasm is fed. And it is within the parish that effective means should be developed to stir up the enthusiasm of parishioners and to coordinate their efforts to be instruments of God's powerful, saving, loving presence throughout the planet.

## Questions for Reflection and Discussion

1. What contemporary expressions help you understand the meaning of "kingdom" as it appears in the Christian Scriptures?

2. How comfortable are you with people seeing or knowing about your good works? The good works of your parish?

3. What features of communes of the 1960s and 1970s seem to have been part of early Christianity?

4. Have ministries in your parish been jeopardized by local conflicts and tensions? If so, how?

5. Is there a healthy mixture of liturgical and non-liturgical ministries in your parish?

# — 3 —

# New Lifestyle and Bias

### Role of Monasteries

In the chaotic times in Europe following the massive movements of peoples called the barbarian invasions (c. 400 C.E.), only a well organized church could sustain and promote the faith. Germanic, Frank, Saxon, Celtic, and Slavic tribes came to baptism with thought patterns and social constructions of reality that clashed with the religious symbolic system of Western Christianity. These were people known for their simplicity, earthiness, realism, and some crudeness. Most came to Christianity by way of mass baptisms, sometimes of whole tribes, without religious formation. This quick transition from paganism to Christianity made it difficult for them to appreciate the religious symbol system already in place that had evolved out of more settled peoples of the Roman Empire. Extreme externalism in religion was a consequence. Sacraments became holy *things* to be received or be touched by, with some overtones of magic. Emphasis was on ministry as something *received* rather than *given*. Religion gravitated toward blessed objects, relics of saints, and devotional practices.

Bishops and priests kept trying to meet the challenges that accompanied this new, massive, different Christian population with traditional ministry. The institutional diocesan church, however, along with other institutional forms in the civil Roman empire, was fighting for survival during what came to be called "the dark ages." A savior was waiting in the wings. Powerful and well organized monasteries had begun to spread through Europe. They found fertile ministry in the distant frontiers of the empire—the Celtic lands of Patrick (385-461) in the British Isles. From there these evangelizing monks crossed over into western Europe.

Although local churches still had their bishops and priests, monasteries, like island havens in stormy seas, became important centers of learning and liturgy in Europe during much of the Middle Ages. In many places they overshadowed the ministry of local clergy. These monasteries took care of the spiritual, physical, cultural, and social needs of the faithful in their neighborhoods. They also sent out missionaries to evangelize those not yet baptized.

These monks and nuns, committed to celibacy and to religious life, lived behind protective walls, and were dedicated to prayer, contemplation, learning, and worship. Their contribution to the church in Europe during those critical years is well recorded. In them ministry had taken an entirely new turn. It was done by women and men who were dedicated to a life that kept them separated from the people they served. Ministry no longer sprang from the people themselves.

Eventually the diocesan church structure collided with the influence of monasteries.

> From an historical perspective the aim of the eventual prohibition by the church of preaching by monks who were not priests was simply to protect the parochial and diocesan structure. . . .the consequence of this opposition was . . . that in the tenth and eleventh centuries all the great abbeys abandoned any pastoral care in the surrounding district; this was reserved for the diocesan clergy (Schillebeeckx, *The Church with a Human Face*, p. 75).

This medieval prohibition against lay preaching, in this case by non-ordained monks, would continue until the new Code of Canon Law in 1983 (Canons 759, 766, 767.1).

## Influence of Celibacy on Ministry

Commitment to a celibate way of life on the part of monks and nuns influenced the lifestyle, discipline, and spirituality of bishops and priests in the Western church and, consequently, their ministry. In early Christianity, ministers could not be distinguished by lifestyle. True, Paul had recommended celibacy and virginity as an ascetical practice for all who could do so because the end times were approaching (1 Corinthians 7:25–26). Writers of our Scriptures recommended that bishops and deacons marry only once (1 Timothy 3:1ff). There is no evidence that a celibate lifestyle of ministers had become widespread during the first generations of Christianity.

The first hints of a distinct lifestyle arose in the 200s when clergy were expected to live differently, especially in regard to sexual expressions and marriage. The Hebrew Scriptures (Leviticus 22:3–6) mandated that their Jewish priests refrain from intercourse before serving at the altar. Once the notion of priesthood had evolved in Christianity, the priesthood of the New Covenant was considered greater than that of the Old Covenant. The call to purity was considered greater, too. And since priests served at the altar all their life, shouldn't their abstinence be permanent?

Early heretics, such as Manichaeans and Montanists, added their negative influence by teaching that all sexual activity—including that of the laity—was impure. Some church leaders, such as St. Augustine, taught that original sin was transmitted through intercourse. Therefore, abstinence and virginity were the ideal lifestyle and only the weak should marry. However, most bishops and presbyters continued to marry.

Priests continued to live in the same style as the people they served. They farmed and worked at trades. They did not wear distinctive clothing. Only bishops, because of their extensive responsibilities, did not do ordinary work, and they wore a distinctive insignia. Beginning in the late fifth century, priests began wearing a long tunic to distinguish them from the laity, who wore a short one. This evolved into the modern cleric's alb and the everyday dark cassock.

The tradition of celibacy continued to evolve. In some places it was expected that priests not be sexually active after ordination. When monastic spirituality became popular in the fourth and fifth centuries, it promoted the ideal of celibacy as a model for all priests. However, the crisis in Europe following the barbarian invasions made it difficult for church leaders to enforce the discipline of clerical celibacy.

One way church authority enforced celibacy was by ordaining monks who were already committed to celibacy and would evangelize large areas of Europe. Church authority continued to mandate celibacy. The First Lateran Council (1123-1153) forbade those in orders to marry and ordered those already married to renounce their wives and do penance. Later legislation declared the marriages of clerics not only illegal but also invalid. Widespread disregard of these laws continued until preparation for priesthood was recognized following the Protestant Reformation and the Council of Trent (1545-1563).

## Exclusion of Women

Except for cloistered nuns and influential abbesses, women came to be excluded from church ministries in most Christian communities. Only during the exciting new times of emerging Christianity did the baptized find freedom in the revelation that in Christ there is "no longer male and female." The gospels, Acts, and Pauline letters witness the fact that women were prominent in ministry during the public life of Jesus and immediately afterward. Jesus refused to be bound by the constraints and prejudices that his patriarchal society, culture—and religion—felt about women. He touched and was touched by them as he carried out his mission.

He moved among them as his equals and made no distinctions, even though his apostles and disciples sometimes wondered about him: "Just then his disciples came. They were astonished that he was speaking with a woman, but no one said, 'What do you want?' or 'Why are you speaking with her?'" (John 4:27). This woman at the well served as an evangelist by taking the good news about Jesus to her village. Jesus had female disciples as well as male and they traveled with him. Women from among the disciples were the primary witnesses at the death of Jesus; they were also the first witnesses to his resurrection:

> . . . and returning from the tomb, they told all this to the eleven and to all the rest. Now it was Mary Magdalene, Joanna, Mary the mother of James, and the other women with them who told this to the apostles. But these words seemed to them an idle tale, and they did not believe them (Luke 24:9ff).

Women were also in the upper room and received the commissioning flames of Pentecost (Acts 1:14).

Why did Jesus take such a revolutionary stand in regard to women?

> The answer has to be found in his own conviction that in his presence there was the inauguration of a new world where God is allowed to be God, and where men and women— children of the same God, his Father—were allowed to be men

and women—brothers and sisters equally (Moloney, *Woman First Among the Faithful*, p. 34).

Ministry in emerging Christianity was an equal opportunity situation because the baptized lived the good news of equality among all of God's sons and daughters. During the time of Paul, women were missionaries of the gospel of Jesus; they were co-workers with the likes of Paul and Barnabas; they were teachers and prophets, headed local communities as benefactors, served as deaconesses, and ministered as widows. The gospel of Jesus was fresh and the Pentecostal Spirit revolutionary. The Scriptures do not clearly describe these ministerial roles of women during those first generations, but neither do they describe the roles of men. As Paul and other authors write to the churches, their greetings, passing references, and use of ministerial action verbs make the role of women evident. For example, between 54-58 C.E. Paul writes to the Christian communities in Rome (women's names emphasized):

I commend to you our sister *Phoebe*, a deacon of the church at Cenchreae, so that you may welcome her in the Lord as is fitting for the saints, and help her in whatever she may require from you, for she has been a benefactor of many and of myself as well.

Greet *Prisca* and Aquila, who work with me in Christ Jesus, and who risked their necks for my life, to whom not only I give thanks, but also the churches of the Gentiles. Greet also the church in their house. Greet my beloved Epaenetus, who was the first convert in Asia for Christ. Greet *Mary*, who has worked very hard among you. Greet Andronicus and *Junia*, my relatives who were in prison with me; they are prominent among the apostles, and they were in Christ before I was. Greet Ampliatus, my beloved in the Lord. Greet Urbanus, our co-worker in Christ, and my beloved Stachys. Greet Apelles, who is approved in Christ. Greet those who belong to the family of Aristobulus. Greet my relative Herodion. Greet those in the Lord who belong to the family of Narcissus. Greet those workers in the Lord, *Tryphaena* and *Tryphosa*. Greet the beloved *Persis*, who has worked hard in the Lord. Greet Rufus, chosen in the Lord; and greet his *mother*—a mother to me also. Greet Asyncritus, Phlegon, Hermes, Patrobas, Hermas, and the brothers and *sisters* who are with them. Greet Philologus, *Julia*,

Hereus and his *sister*, and Olympas, and all the saints who are with them. Greet one another with a holy kiss. All the churches of Christ greet you (Romans 16:1ff).

The exact meaning of descriptive phrases used by the Scripture writers is not always easy to recover. Part of the reason is that the role of women in the early church was ignored for centuries and therefore not considered by theologians. Elisabeth Schüssler Fiorenza writes about Phoebe, whom Paul greeted as a deacon and as his *benefactor*:

> The importance of Phoebe's position as minister in the church at Cenchreae is underlined by the title *prostatis*, usually translated "helper" or "patroness," although in the literature of the time the term has the connotation of leading officer, president, governor, or superintendent. Since Paul claims that Phoebe was a *prostatis* of many and also of Paul himself, scholars reject such a meaning here. However, in 1 Thessalonians 5:12 the verb characterizes persons with authority in the community and in 1 Timothy 3:4ff and 5:17 it designates the functions of the bishop, deacon, or elder (*In Memory of Her*, p. 181).

After Paul's time it did not take long for sins of prejudice and the powerful discriminating influence of culture to close the door on women's public involvement in both church ministries and civil society. Catholicism emerged from those ancient times with officially recognized ministry restricted to men—ordained men. Early fathers of the church and medieval church leaders and theologians continued to justify the inferiority of women. As the Middle Ages approached modern times, another motive for the exclusion of women surfaced:

> . . . by the mid-thirteenth century there are clear signs of the masculine suspicions and intolerance that one finds so dramatically expressed a bit later in the trial of Joan of Arc. What is difficult to say is whether this anti-feminism is the logical outgrowth of much earlier currents of thought (e.g., the negativity toward women present in much monastic literature) or is rather an aspect of the wave of intolerance that came in as a reaction to Albigensianism, the Waldenses, and like movements. . . .Whatever its roots, the relegation of women to doubly sec-

ond-class status in the church (they were not only laity, they were not even laymen) was so effective that it remained almost unchallenged to the present day (Cooke, *Ministry to Word and Sacraments*, p. 115).

Emphasis upon celibacy after the sixth century contributed to a negative attitude in church leadership toward all women and sealed a bias against their involvement in any official church ministry. In the official perception, close association with women, often considered seducers and temptresses, threatened the celibacy and chastity of clergy and monks. While the positive value of freely chosen celibacy and chastity ranks high in true Catholic tradition, it often promoted a *separatist* pattern of behavior in church ministry.

## Transition to Modern Times

It was not unusual for bishops and priests to be preoccupied with rank and privilege during the Middle Ages. This scandalous tendency, often a curse of clericalism, increased during the age of Feudalism. The unranked and somewhat messy charismatic gifts in early Christianity had been replaced with a well-defined hierarchical pyramid by the thirteenth century: bishop (on top), then priests, religious, and on the bottom the ordinary laity. Lifestyle, too, was graded according to these ranks. Both the universal and local church itself was seen in this pyramidal way. A religious class system had developed.

This new structure in Catholicism had repercussions on the very meaning of ministry, which was reduced to priesthood, and even more narrowly to eucharistic ritual. It became identified with an *office*, or position, in the church, rather than with a charism. Along with this clerical office came a special power—a supernatural power—within the sacramental order. This power was conferred through the laying on of hands, called the ritual of ordination. Since earliest times this had been a simple ritual of designating a person for the responsibility of leadership.

The Latin term *ordo*, or order, was predicated of all clerics. While in its origin the term simply meant any organized group, it had come to define those men ordained and set apart to deal with *the sacred*. The laity, on the other hand, dealt with *profane*, or worldly, matters only.

Great and holy saints could be found among bishops and priests. Many, however, were ordained with minimal religious formation and few or no gifts for ministry. It was not unusual that clergy were mere functionaries of sacred sacramental rituals and of blessing of things for protection against physical and supernatural evils. Incidents of corruption and failure in ministry were common. Desire for internal reform on the part of the church's leadership, from Rome down to the most insignificant village, was lacking.

Then came the reformers in the sixteenth century. They wanted to reform the church and ministry by returning to the spirit, theological emphases, and ecclesial forms of early Christianity. In the process they discovered that there would be chaos if everyone was equally a minister or priest. They, like Paul in first-generation Christianity, discovered the perils of undisciplined charisms. Eventually some Protestant reformation traditions limited ministry even more than it was limited in the Catholic parish; they restricted it to the *pastor.*

From the time of the reformers in the sixteenth century the terms "ministry" and "minister"would be associated with Protestants. Seldom was it used by Catholics before Vatican II.

At the Council of Trent (1545-1563), Catholic leadership reacted to Protestant reform movements by placing even more emphasis on its hierarchical structure and priestly powers. The central authority of the Vatican was further developed, becoming ever more monarchical. The quality of priestly ministry improved through the establishment of tightly regulated seminaries. Special ministries in the church, especially its missionary work and service to immigrant churches, were done by religious communities, with new ones being founded every year.

All seemed to be working well in a highly controlled way.

## Questions for Reflection and Discussion

1. If ministry is so thoroughly influenced by culture, where do you see that influence today?

2. Do you feel ministry benefitted by the requirement of celibacy? Explain.

3. How did cultural factors at the beginning and in later times prevent women from assuming ministerial roles?

# — 4 —

# Renewal of
# Lay Ministry

**Running Full Circle**

So far we have glided quickly though the pages of the history of pre-Vatican II ministry. We also reflected briefly on emerging Christianity's grasp of ministry as being instruments of the loving and saving presence of God—the reign of God. We cannot remain in the past; we minister in our own times. Depending upon our own insights, commitments, and biases, we can describe these new times by pouncing on half of Dickens's famous beginning of *A Tale of Two Cities:* "It was the best of times, it was the worst of times."

Over the past thirty years most Catholic parishes have experienced what has been called an "explosion" of ministries. Church leadership did not deliberately create new and more effective ways of serving a global Catholic community approaching a billion members. No. Catholic men and women once again began to claim their dignity and responsibility as initiated—baptized—members of the local Catholic church. We might very well feel closer to the spirit-filled Christians of Jerusalem, Antioch, Alexandria, and Ephesus of apostolic times than we do to the monks and nuns of the Middle Ages, than to the vowed religious men and women of modern times, than to the parishioners of clergy-run parishes of the past 1800 years. We have come full circle, so to speak. We enjoy a grace of new beginnings, new times. The reign of God is always current.

## Vatican Council II

Shifts in the way we understand the mystery of church and the mystery of our contemporary world ushered in new times. Bishops and their theologians at Vatican II (1962-1965) reflected on the Scriptures and centuries of tradition. They included in their reflections and discussions insights gained from evidence of the presence of God still acting in current cultures. By the end of the council, they had signed documents that cultivated a renewal of diversity of ministries and laid the foundation for new times in the church. Of critical importance to ministry are the Dogmatic Constitution on the Church *(Lumen Gentium)*, Pastoral Constitution on the Church in the Modern World *(Gaudium et Spes)*, and Decree on the Apostolate of the Laity *(Apostolicam Actuositatem)*.

Key to renewed lay ministry is the council's definition of the church as the "people of God." The council fathers devoted the entire Chapter II of *Lumen Gentium* to this description of the church as the new people of God. This scriptural image emphasizes the human and communal nature of the church rather than its institutional and hierarchical dimensions. All the baptized are members of a community. All share in the threefold ministry of Jesus as prophet, priest, and king. This threefold designation describes a responsibility—and privilege—to share the revealing and saving Word of God, to share mediating responsibilities between God and people, and to share in leadership responsibilities. Lay and ordained are not fenced off from each other. Nor are they corralled into one or other layer of a holy pyramid, with dignity and responsibility parceled out according to rank. As baptized people of God, regardless of being lay or ordained, we are called to service— though not necessarily the same service—precisely because we are baptized:

> For their sacred pastors know how much the laity contribute to the welfare of the entire Church. Pastors also know that they themselves were not meant by Christ to shoulder alone the entire saving mission of the Church toward the world. On the contrary, they understand that it is their noble duty so to shepherd the faithful and to recognize their services and charismatic gifts that all according to their proper roles may cooperate in this common undertaking with one heart *(Lumen Gentium, 30)*.

Lay ministry is not simply a participation in what properly belongs to bishops and priests. Nor is it a stop-gap activity in the absence of the ordained. It belongs to the laity by reason of their initiation sacraments of baptism, confirmation, and eucharist:

> [Laity and pastors] are bound together by a mutual need. Pastors of the church, following the example of the Lord, should minister to one another and to the faithful. The faithful in their turn should enthusiastically lend their cooperative assistance to their pastors and teachers *(Lumen Gentium*, 32).

The exciting use of the descriptive phrase "people of God" was compromised twenty years later at the Extraordinary Synod of 1985. Bishops of the world were called together to commemorate the twentieth anniversary of Vatican II. Some objected that the description of the church as the "people of God" overshadowed other traditional descriptions of the church, such as the Body of Christ. There was concern, too, that the phrase encouraged democratic thinking in the church, such as people were used to in civic affairs. While the synod did reemphasize the collegial spirit of Vatican II, commitment to consensus resulted in the elimination of the phrase "people of God" from the document, except for its use in the title, *A Message to the People of God and the Final Report.* (See Dulles, *The Reshaping of Catholicism,* pp. 184-193.)

Terminology that comes so easily to the tongue thirty years after the council hardly appears in Vatican II documents, especially "lay ministry." By the early 1960s a new terminology that had already evolved before World War II became commonplace. The most familiar was "lay apostolate." Therefore, the use of such descriptions as "apostolic activity of the People of God" could be considered as affirming the laity. Interestingly, the Scriptures used by the council documents as examples of this lay apostolate in the early church include missionary work, evangelization, and the mention of women and deaconesses (see *Apostolicam Actuositatem,* 1).

Even Vatican II was not ready to tackle what had evolved after the earliest generations of the church and had been carved in stone since the Council of Trent, namely, the authority and prestige belonging to those who were ordained as bishops and priests. To them belonged ministry in its proper sense of priesthood and leadership. However, the council did affirm all Catholic people's full stature in the church. It once again broadened the notion of ministry to include service beyond that of the ordained clergy. It also shed, at least in word, the triumphalism that had been associated with its hierarchy.

## Defining Ministry

Because language reflects reality and can even shape it, the popular use of "minister" and "ministry" has caused considerable anxiety for some church officials and parishioners in the years following Vatican II. Many are reluctant and even refuse to associate these terms with women and men who are not ordained. For almost eighteen hundred years "ministry" had been closely associated with the "priesthood" and canonical authority of the male clergy in the local church. Their rights, responsibilities, and jurisdiction came by way of ordination and were clearly identified in church law and local practice.

Christians of New Testament times had a different notion of ministry, sometimes using a simple Greek secular word *diakonia* to describe the great variety of good deeds that was expected of the baptized. This word is translated into English as "service" or "ministry," but it had many concrete meanings in New Testament times. Among them is waiting on table, actually a service normally performed by slaves. The seven men who are called to distribute food in Acts 6:1ff are called to *diakonia*, to service, to ministry, probably to some administrative activity associated with the tables—not to the ordained office of deacons or diaconate. Soon the term was used more broadly to describe activities that benefitted the community in some loving way. Sometimes early Christians used the term *charis*, translated by "charism" or "gift," to describe what we popularly call "ministry." Or they used a descriptive word such as "teacher" or "prophet."

Christians of New Testament times would be totally confused by our use of "laity" to describe the baptized who are not ordained. They had no such distinction among themselves. All the baptized were the new *laos*, or people, the new people of God, a people who were neither ". . . Jew or Greek . . . slave or free . . . male and female; for all of you are one in Christ Jesus" (Galatians 3:28). If they could have seen our current preoccupations and anxieties, they might have included "neither lay nor ordained!"

This distinction between lay and ordained, however, continues in current church law. Even the highest authorities in the church continue to be reluctant to predicate the word "ministry" of lay persons, distinguishing sharply between the ordained ministry proper to priests, and other "services" that may sometimes be rendered by lay people. This attitude prefers to regard these "services" as a transient emergency alternative solution, which will no longer be needed when there are enough priestly vocations (*National Catholic Reporter*, May 6, 1994).

Our American bishops chose not to make an issue of reserving the term "ministry" to the ordained. In *Called and Gifted: The American Catholic Laity* (1980), they state:

> Baptism and confirmation empower all believers to share in some form of ministry. Although the specific form of participation in ministry varies according to the gifts of the Holy Spirit, all who share in this work are united with one another. "Just as each of us has one body with many members, and not all the members have the same function, so too we, though many, are one body in Christ and individually members of one another. We have gifts that differ according to the favor bestowed on each of us" (Romans 12:4–6). This unity in ministry should be especially evident in the relationships between laity and clergy as lay men and women respond to the call of the Spirit in their lives. The clergy help to call forth, identify, coordinate, and affirm the diverse gifts bestowed by the Spirit. We applaud this solidarity between laity and clergy as their most effective ministry and witness to the world (p. 4).

Ministry as predicated of either clergy or laity should not be limited to either church (ecclesial) or liturgical activities. It must always reflect its most primal meaning of being the instrument of God's saving presence—God's reign, which is not synonymous with church and sanctuary.

Thomas O'Meara, O.P., offers a comprehensive definition of ministry that avoids restricting it to ecclesial and/or liturgical functions of the ordained. Wishing to be accurate and precise, he defines ministry as having six characteristics.

> Ministry is: 1) doing something; 2) for the advent of the kingdom; 3) in public; 4) on behalf of a Christian community; 5) which is a gift received in faith, baptism and ordination; and which is 6) an activity with its own limits and identity within a diversity of ministerial actions (*Theology of Ministry*, p. 136).

Taking all of this into consideration, when can we say that activity done by a baptized Catholic is truly ministry? A final answer is still not totally evident in current writing. The ministry experience of both lay women and men, along with that of the ordained, will contribute to a continuing evolution of a definition. In the meantime, we can summarize O'Meara's six characteristics into two key elements. Ministry is present 1) when the baptized person's activity makes explicit God's power and presence in some way, a public activity which is, therefore, gospel- and kingdom-oriented; 2) when a baptized person is chosen, or delegated, or commissioned, or ordained by the community to perform this activity.

Ministry, therefore, is not some free-floating activity that people take upon themselves without consideration of or contact with the Catholic community. While all the baptized are called to be disciples and to do good deeds, not all good deeds are ministry or service or *diakonia*. As we will see below, lay ministers often have identifiable titles and job descriptions. (See "New Kids on the Block," Chapter 5.)

## Tensions in Ministry

Before we leave this theme of renewal of lay ministry, we should acknowledge the presence of tensions related to lay ministry that often exist in Catholic parishes. This kind of tension is not new to Catholicism and should not be an insurmountable obstacle to pastoral care. As we saw in Chapter 1, at the beginning of the church there was often sharp tension between Jew and Gentile Christians and within groups representative of both. There was tension in ministry between some men and women and Paul. Later tensions prompted community leaders to limit the role of women. There were disputes between presbyters and deacons. During the Middle Ages there was competition between diocesan clergy and monks taking pastoral care of people, with lay monks eventually forbidden to preach. A little later in the Middle Ages there was conflict between diocesan clergy and popular mendicant orders such as Dominicans and Franciscans as each went about providing pastoral care. Quite often bishops and even the highest leadership in Rome got involved in the disputes.

If today we experience occasions of conflict and "turf wars" on the part of traditional priests and lay pastoral ministers, we should take a deep breath and be assured that this, too, shall pass, but that other tensions will be around the corner.

## Questions for Reflection and Discussion

1. How has your parish experienced an explosion of new ministries?

2. Why would Vatican II's use of "people of God" influence attitudes toward ministry?

3. Why would there be controversy surrounding a term such as "ministry?"

4. Has your parish experienced conflicts between clergy and lay pastoral leaders? Why? Over what?

# — 5 —

# A Paradigm Shift

### Prosumer Parish

Actual examples from the daily life of a lay parish administrator illustrate the paradigm shift in how we understand Catholic ministry today. We have entered a new era in the Catholic church when ministry done by the non-ordained is critical for parish life, as we see from the following.

> The rectory phone rings. The caller says that her mother is home recuperating from surgery and asks if someone from the parish can bring communion to her. I ask if she or some other family member would like to do so. She is very pleased that this is possible. So I ask her to meet me after Mass to receive a pyx for the consecrated bread which she can bring to Mass with her in the future. I also give her instructions for this eucharistic ministry.
>
> After Mass a man asks about someone from the parish bringing communion to his father, but he is not comfortable doing so himself. There is no other family member able or willing to do so. I assign one of our regular eucharistic ministers to do this.
>
> Janet, who is a eucharistic minister, brought communion for many months to her neighbor, Bill, who was terminally ill. It took his wife, Shirley, and me a long time to convince Bill that it was a good thing to receive communion from a lay person, and that a priest was not available in our parish for ministry to the homebound. This was hard for him to understand, and it

took him a while to accept the idea of receiving communion from me or from any commissioned eucharistic minister.

Several years later, Shirley herself became terminally ill, and the same neighbor brought her communion, too, and a precious ministry relationship was formed between the two. They had discovered in a very personal way that God can touch our lives and grace us through one another. This doesn't happen only through an ordained priest.

Another example of parishioners taking care of the needs of one another is our Area Center for Emergency Relief where food and clothing are distributed. It has a volunteer director and part-time staff, plus a board of directors representing participating churches. This center gives year-round help to area residents in emergency situations, including occasional fuel or housing needs for residents or transients. Donations are received from area residents and organizations. There is also some diocesan funding from Operation Rice Bowl. This center also coordinates seasonal donations of food and gifts from schools, businesses, and churches.

Still another way parishioners minister to one another's needs, this time their spiritual needs, is our Befriender program. This program originated at the Saint Paul Seminary School of Divinity of the College of St. Thomas in St. Paul, Minnesota. Parish coordinators are trained over a period of a week of 20-30 hours.

In the Befriender ministry, parishioners are trained to listen and to give one-on-one support to other parishioners who are going through a particularly difficult time in their life: sickness, terminal illness, bereavement, death of a spouse or a child, divorce, etc. It is primarily a ministry of listening, personal support, and friendship. It is not a counseling or an errand service or other direct service. Befrienders are not expected to solve problems but simply to listen and to offer support while the person works through a particular burden.

These are a few examples of a subtle but profound shift that is gradually taking place in parish life. Although we feel, with these examples, that we are moving rapidly forward, we are actually stepping back in time to the early years of the church. Then believers commonly knew that they were the Body of Christ and that the various gifts and ministries of the church were distributed among them by the Spirit of God to be used to build up the Body in unity and strength.

Parishioners are no longer only on the receiving end of ministry. They are also participants in the actual *doing* of ministry as a normal style of parish life. We might call the contemporary parish a "prosumer" parish. This notion was developed by Alvin Toffler in *The Third Wave* (William Morrow, 1980) in describing a new concept in economics:

> . . . whether we look at self-help movements, do-it-yourself trends, or new production technologies, we find the same shift toward a much closer involvement of the consumer in production. In such a world, conventional distinctions between producer and consumer vanish. The "outsider" becomes an "insider," and even more production is shifted from Sector B of the economy to Sector A where the prosumer reigns. As this occurs we begin—glacially at first but then, perhaps with accelerating speed—to alter that most fundamental of our institutions: the market (p. 292).

Change the last word "market" to "parish" and we understand better what has happened in our generation. Ours is a movement from parishioners as "consumers" to parishioners actively involved in a host of ministries or enjoying what they themselves produce: "prosumers." This represents a major shift in the normal style of being parish: from hundreds of years of being very much the receivers of ministry from ordained priests only, or in recent centuries from vowed religious women and men in schools and other institutional settings such as hospitals.

This proliferation of ministries of parishioners within parishes is becoming so much a part of modern church life that it is difficult to visualize a time when it was not so. Yet that other time is still a recent memory. As one minister recalls:

> I remember when I first came to my current parish assignment as a pastoral administrator, the people looked at me as the "doer" of all the ministries, rather than the coordinator and facilitator of the parish's ministries. They viewed their role as "helping" me with what I was supposed to do. The big shift

had supposedly already happened, namely, that a lay woman was now doing much of what had been done in the past by an ordained priest, and still is in most parishes. This is a major change but still is a far cry from actual ownership of the parish ministry by the parishioners themselves as "prosumers."

The "prosumer" parish is not a concept that is understood, accepted, and implemented instantly. It takes months and years of patience for this to happen as people gradually discover their gifts and their call to serve the Body of Christ who they themselves are.

Another difficulty in becoming a prosumer parish is that it comes into head-on conflict with the cultural context of a consumer society. For centuries, people have been programmed to come to the parish as they would to a bank or a grocery store or any other institution to receive goods and services in exchange for the least amount of money or effort possible. This kind of underlying attitude also needs to be discussed up front with parishioners and those seeking membership in the parish. Continuing to be a "consumer" parish makes formation of a true community all but impossible. In fact, to cater to the "consumer" parish attitude is a form of selling out the gospel call to the pressures of the culture, and it denies people an authentic experience of church as community, not just an institution.

The concept of a prosumer parish versus a consumer parish is readily understood and accepted by people. The major challenge is working it out in day-to-day parish life when we are constantly competing with the rest of society for our parishioners' time and attention. Also, many people prefer the "old" way, when little was asked of them in terms of parish involvement beyond attendance at Sunday Mass.

## New Kids on the Block

While Vatican II stands as a clear symbol of these new times in the Catholic church, making paradigm shifts in parish ministries possible, it was not the single direct cause of these new times for Catholics. Rather, it was one of many world events in the late 1900s associated with massive shifts in societies and cultures. These shifts contributed to new directions in Catholic ministry. Authority in traditional institutions such as schools, governments, and churches has been questioned. There have been class struggles, civil rights movements, a women's movement, condemnation of some "isms," and the invention of others. All in all, there has been some chaos and there have been exciting new possibilities.

The local Catholic parish is not immune from the anxieties and crises of these new times. Beginning in the mid to late 1960s new forms of ministries evolved quickly. First there was a questioning of the priorities of parochial schools, their finances, and personnel. This coincided with a pullback of religious communities from staffing schools due to their own personnel shortage and commitment to new priorities. One school after another was closed. A religious formation vacuum created by these closings needed to be filled. While the CCD (Confraternity of Christian Doctrine) had been officially in place in most parishes for generations, a more comprehensive formation was needed. In the late 1960s parishes began hiring full-time religious education directors, soon to be called Directors, or Coordinators, of Religious Education (DREs/CREs).

Other full-time or part-time "parish ministers" soon followed: liturgists, pastoral ministers, youth ministers, and other specialists. Graduate schools associated with religious colleges and universities provided the education and formation needed for these special ministries. Because few parishioners were ready for these new opportunities, these new ministers were often hired from outside the parish, from outside the diocese, and even from outside the state. For the first time a process of interview and contract negotiation became part of Catholic ministry.

As Catholic parishes continued to chart new directions, new ministry positions evolved, sometimes new titles for ministries already in place, for example, pastoral ministers and pastoral associates. A growing shortage of clergy prompted creative planning with pastoral administrators, or lay parish directors, coming on the scene.

The first wave of these new ministers was mostly women and men in religious communities, many of whom had served in other ministries previously. Not long afterwards, non-religious women and men entered graduate schools and other special formation programs in preparation for full-time parish ministry. In recent years there has been still another source of parish workers: hiring parishioners themselves for what professionally trained women and men had previously been hired to do. This choice is usually associated with parish economics and financial priorities.

Ministry specialists are not the only new kids on the block. The reform of Catholic liturgy meant that parishioners would be invited to take their place in the sanctuary as readers and ministers of the

Eucharist. Parish structure was also enhanced with the formation of parish councils, commissions, and committees. The ministry of leadership, previously reserved to the ordained pastor, was now shared with parishioners, though by church law the pastor remained in charge over all aspects of parish life and ministry. The renewal of the catechumenate (RCIA) called for special formation teams and sponsors. Parish bulletins today describe other ministries in the typical Catholic parish.

Parish life is also vitalized by the many parishioners who, while not identified as ministers in a strict sense, are dissatisfied with a merely passive membership and attendance at Sunday Mass. Their faith commitment urges them to be involved and give witness to their faith. For this reason they are involved in outreach efforts among the poor, responding to housing crises, family crises, and a variety of other opportunities to answer the gospel call to service.

Many women and men choose one or other of the church's ministries as their life's work or career, by which they support themselves and their families. Some form of contract binds them to a particular church community for a certain length of time. Since "professionalism" is prevalent in our culture, expecting and even demanding certain levels of education and credentials for leadership positions, these ministers are sometimes called professional church workers because they have earned professional credentials, often one or more graduate degrees and/or certification through diocesan formation processes.

A better insight into ministry as a "profession" might come from the use of this word in religious communities of women and men. For them, "profession" was the ritual of full commitment—professing commitment—for a specific length of time (temporary profession) or for life (final, or permanent, profession). Since commissioning rituals are popular in parish ministry, a special ritual of "profession" might give to the full-time and contracted minister a more precise identity.

Not all ministries are of equal importance, duration, or intensity. A eucharistic minister at Sunday Mass is truly a minister, but not as critical for the community as is the pastor who presides. A director of the catechumenate is closer to the heart of the church's mission than is the altar server. The parishioner who visits the homebound reflects the meaning of ministry more intensely than a member of the art and environment committee.

## Questions for Reflection and Discussion

1. How has your parish moved from being a "consumer" parish to being a "prosumer" parish? Reflect on the examples of parishioners actually taking part in ministry in your parish.

2. How many "new kids on the block" are evident in your parish ministries compared to 1970? Who are they?

3. In your experience, are parishioners enthusiastic to answer the gospel call to service? Why? Why not?

# — 6 —

# Signs
# of the Times

## Effect of Shortage of Priests
## and Lay Parish Administrators

It is a fact of the current Catholic scene that a shortage of ordained priests is accelerating. Approximately ten percent of U.S. parishes are without a resident priest pastor. This shortage always was the situation in some parts of the church, especially in mission lands. Now it is more the rule than the exception in established churches of the Western world. While lay ministry is a right and responsibility of every baptized Catholic, this shortage of priests has made lay ministry not only more acceptable but also necessary. Sharing ministry with the laity only because of a crisis situation, however, misunderstands both the nature of ministry and God's people:

> Theological discussions about shared ministries have to begin with the assumption that a sharing community already exists. The shared ministry, like the shared bread and cup, will simply be one more sign or sacrament of a sharing community. Where the bread is not shared, there is no Christian community. That's simple enough. Shared ministry begins, not with a downward distribution of the pie of authority by ordained ministers, but with the recognition and celebration of the gifts of the baptized who share "all things in common," including ministry. Of course such shared ministries will gradually include some kind of order that of necessity comes from

unity with the larger church. Without such an ordering toward the larger communion, a local community would eventually become a sect, following its own "charismatic" leader (Rademacher, *Lay Ministry*, p. 170).

The shortage of ordained priests has added new dimensions to lay ministry. More and more lay women and men are being assigned by bishops to full-time liturgical and administrative roles in parishes. Diocese after diocese searches for ways that parishes can work toward being ministerially complete in the absence of an ordained priest. Some dioceses are clustering parishes so that fewer priests can minister to more parishes. Others are assigning a pastoral administrator, or pastoral coordinator, sometimes called a lay parish director, who is responsible for the day-to-day operations of a parish. Some of these are women or men under religious vows; others are lay women or men. In this scenario, an ordained sacramental minister is responsible for presiding at Mass and sacraments. Philip Murnion, director of the National Parish Life Center in New York City, praises dioceses that have lay parish directors: "I think they tend to take a planning approach to parish ministry, as opposed to a kind of adaptive approach. They anticipate situations, then set up a process."

These special ministries in parishes without an ordained priest flow from Canon 517.2 of the 1983 Code of Canon Law:

If the diocesan bishop should decide that due to a dearth of priests a participation in the exercise of the pastoral care of a parish is to be entrusted to a deacon or to some other person who is not a priest or to a community of persons, he is to appoint some priest endowed with the powers and faculties of a pastor to supervise the pastoral care.

Under the former Code of Canon Law, a parish had to have a priest pastor appointed by the local bishop. A parish that did not have a resident pastor was designated as a "mission." That has changed.

The new code creates two new positions: that of a lay person who can be responsible for sharing in the pastoral care of a parish, through canonical appointment by the bishop, and that of a priest who, while not resident in the parish, has supervisory functions over the lay person in residence. The code, however, does not give these persons specific titles. . . .These two working together are responsible for the pastoral care of a parish. . . .It is highly probable that the position of lay pastor will have enormous impact in virtually every diocese in the United States within the next ten to twenty years. Thus it is essential that we understand it theologically and implement it properly, with due regard to parochial sensitivity and the norms of canon law (Chandler, *The Pastoral Associate and the Lay Pastor*, pp. 52, 59).

Each bishop must deal with the effects of the priest shortage in his own diocese. The way canon 517.2 is interpreted and applied varies somewhat from diocese to diocese. The title of the lay administrator also varies. Titles currently in use are: pastoral administrator, pastoral minister, lay pastor, non-ordained pastor, pastoral coordinator, pastoral life coordinator, parochial minister. The title given the priest assigned to sacramental ministry in a parish with a non-ordained pastoral leader also varies from diocese to diocese.

A number of studies have been done on this growing phenomenon. A recent one by NACPA (National Association of Church Personnel Administrators) found approximately 300 lay pastoral leaders scattered throughout the country, and the number is growing steadily. This study also found that there was no formal way for them to organize themselves or network beyond their local groups. It has offered to assist local lay administrators in this effort.

Because the designation of lay administrators of a parish is new, some solutions may seem more radical than others. For example, the following is a description of a lay parish minister in the Netherlands:

On the evening before Pentecost, Esther Nelemans donned her cream-colored liturgical robe and led the worship service at St. Aloysius Catholic Church in Utrecht.

The 32-year-old woman broke bread over the altar, read from the Bible and gave a talk about the meaning of the Tower of Babel. Before the hour-long ceremony was over she also distributed Communion and led the singing.

Nelemans is part of Dutch Catholicism's answer to the priest shortage.

She is one of 596 lay pastoral workers authorized by the bishops for pastoral ministry in parishes, hospitals and prisons and to hold offices in church service agencies normally reserved for priests.

More than 200 of the lay workers are women, part of a 25-year-old program that began when lay people crowded university theology departments, although they did not want to become priests.

Now, on priestless weekends many lay pastoral workers lead special prayer services that parallel the Mass, but without the consecration of bread and wine. At many, pre-consecrated hosts are distributed.

These are called Word and Communion services while the Mass is called a eucharistic celebration.

More than half of the lay workers are active in parish ministry. They receive the same theological training from Catholic universities as priesthood candidates and are paid an average monthly salary of almost $3000 (Catholic News Service, quoted in *The Catholic Weekly*, June 10, 1994).

## Prominence of Women

It should not be surprising that women are prominent in ministries of all forms today—except for priesthood and diaconate. Women have filled the ranks of parish volunteers for generations. It was only natural that they continue to do so as parish ministries began to evolve in the late 1960s. Previously they had filled the ranks of full-time ministry but under other titles such as school teachers, nurses, social workers, administrators of schools, orphanages, hospitals, and colleges. Many of these women were professed members of religious communities. Beginning in the late 1960s, these traditional ministries were joined by parish ministries, often with administrative responsibilities.

It is of interest to observe the relationship between these two facts: 1) Lay ministries are often volunteer situations or positions with very low financial compensation. 2) The prominence of women in the ranks of volunteers and non-ordained ministries. It leads one to wonder if there is a direct relationship between the prominence of women in positions with very low or no compensation, and whether that is a positive feature or questionable development.

It did not take long for women to challenge the sexist discrimination that Catholic tradition had taken regarding women since the early centuries of Christianity. Many insisted that church authorities affirm the personhood and total equality of women, instead of ignoring the issue or dealing with it in a way that offends women's human and religious experience. They began to urge church authorities and parish congregations to

> . . . think and act in new ways, to choose imagination over the violence of authoritarian structures of power, prestige, and caste . . . not just to permit thinking in new ways but to lead in this thought, to demonstrate that the power of the Christian gospel is strong enough to reverse the patterns of secular history where "no oppressor ever willingly handed over what he thinks is power" (Carr, *Transforming Grace*, p. 35).

Complete honesty about the nature of women and their equal place within the church community soon raised the question of their ordination: Why the calculated, centuries-long exclusion? Here is one major benefit that would result from the ordination of women.

> The correlation of the church's tradition with the experience of women might result in a new understanding of the church as sacrament. As the sacrament of the incarnation of Christ into all of humankind, the church would fittingly express the mutuality of the human sexes and its service to both women and men by male and female ordination. If both men and women participated in all its ministries, it would be a fuller sacrament of the one priesthood of Christ in the whole People of God and of the apostolic witness of the message of Jesus to both men and women. It would be a clearer sacrament of transformation of the priesthood from medieval clerical caste to the New Testament patterns of equality and mutuality that began to be reincorporated into church structures at Vatican Council II . . . (Carr, p. 36)

Carr claims that instead of undermining our tradition of priesthood or adopting all of its "caste" dimension, the ordination of women

> . . . would further the transformation of the priesthood: by admission of those who have traditionally only served, the sign will be clear. It would help to transform the ministry from a predominantly cultic role to a ministerial one, from a symbol

of prestige to a symbol of service, releasing the imagination of half the church's population into fuller operation as the church moves into the future. . . .those women who have led a community in prayer on campuses, in homes for the aged, in hospitals, prisons, or neighborhoods, those who have enabled retreatants in their own discovery of God or the experience of reconciliation recognize that the ability to celebrate the eucharistic meal, to baptize new life into the church, to give absolution, is the appropriate sacramental expression of the liberating action of Christ's grace in their ministries. For the Catholic tradition, in which sacramental experience is central, the ordination of women would be a sign of the church's attentiveness to the concrete experience of its people, of its awareness of where God's grace is working in people (Carr, p. 40).

The leading authorities of the Catholic church in the Vatican have not agreed with this conviction. Already in 1976 the Vatican's Congregation for the Doctrine of Faith tried to quiet discussions about the ordination of women (*Inter Insigniores*, "Declaration on the Question of the Admission of Women to the Ministerial Priesthood," AAS 69, 1977: 98-116). The discussion, however, has become even more widespread. In 1976 the Pontifical Biblical Commission stated that it could find no scriptural evidence that would exclude women from ordination (*Origins*, July 1, 1976).

However, on May 30, 1994, Pope John Paul II emphasized again the church's ban on women priests, stating clearly that this ban is definitive and not open to debate among Catholics. In this apostolic letter to the world's bishops, "On Reserving Priestly Ordination to Men Alone," he declared "that the church has no authority whatsoever to confer priestly ordination on women and that this judgment is to be definitively held by all the church's faithful. . . ." At the same time the pope denies that the all-male priesthood represents any kind of discrimination against women. It is, he would say, Christ's plan for the church. Yet the presence and role of women in church ministry remains absolutely necessary and irreplaceable.

Is this the final chapter in the tense and sometimes bitter disagreement between those who believe that Catholic women should be ordained if that is their desire and calling and they are otherwise qualified, and those who continue to block their ordination, maintaining that the church has no authority to ordain them? Many in ministry feel that this story is not yet finished.

## Illusion of Security

This is an exciting time to be a lay minister, but it is also a very challenging time. Church structures regarding personnel administration have not kept pace with the shifts that have occurred from ministry by priests and religious to that by lay ministers. This lack of structure and procedure concerning job security, just salary, areas of responsibility, and the ramifications of moving from one ministry position to another in the same or different diocese create considerable stress. If structures are in place, they often are hopelessly inadequate for the professionally prepared lay minister who plans to stay in ministry until retirement.

There is also an illusion of security for ministers recruited from within a parish and prepared for parish ministry. What happens if a new pastor wants to replace this minister with someone else? What if this minister feels called to move on to a different parish or a different ministry? Trends in reshaping ministry opportunities also threaten basic economic security of full-time lay ministers. One such trend is to reshape a full-time position with benefits held by a credentialed lay person into several part-time positions without benefits using non-credentialed lay persons.

The structures and processes in place today are still inadequate to meet a host of new challenges. Navigating these stressful issues successfully still depends almost entirely on the creativity, coping skills, and good judgment of the individual parish minister, rather than on dependable policies of the local, diocesan, or national church.

## Questions for Reflection and Discussion

1. How has the shortage of priests affected your parish?

2. Is the presence of women evident in your parish ministries? Diocesan ministries? If so, how? If not, why not?

3. What positive features would female priests contribute to parish life? Any negative features?

4. Are lay ministers in your experience treated with justice and dignity? If so, in what ways? If not, why not?

# PART TWO

# Taking
# an Honest Look
# at Our Identity

# — 7 —

# Ministering
# in a Human Church

## Human from the Beginning

The church has always been a healthy mixture of the human and divine. Both the universal church and the local church are divine mystery enfleshed—incarnated—in human persons. Ministry springs from this mixed source. This has been true since the very first days behind closed doors when apostles and disciples, men and women, trembled in fear and confusion about the Jesus movement that had just ground to a bloody halt on Calvary after just three short years. Weeks later behind the same closed doors, this group, refreshed with experiences of the risen Lord, awaited the promised one, another advocate—the Spirit.

This original church assembly began new times of God's reign with exciting good news, but without charts and blueprints. Undoubtedly they stumbled through their first agenda. High on the list was the need to replace Judas. They felt it important to bring the number of key disciples to twelve again. But why did they choose Matthias to fill out the inner circle rather than Joseph, a.k.a. Barsabbas, a.k.a. Justus, who was also considered for the assignment? (Acts 1:21–26)

Although the choice was interpreted later and included in the Christian Scriptures as the result of divine intervention through the casting of lots (Luke wrote Acts almost 50 years after the events recorded), we might suspect that something quite human was also mixed in the formula, too earthy to record for all times. Did Matthias lobby successfully for the honor? Or was he more popular with key people in the group, or a more charismatic speaker? Or was it something as simple as a more dynamic personality? On the other hand, did Joseph have a problem of tipping too many flagons of wine? Or more serious yet, had he taken more than one tunic while a missionary intern sent out by Jesus?

This interpretation of a scripture scenario might sound a bit facetious. However, it seems to fit the human dimension of the church that has been proven over and over in history.

The conviction that many people have of the origins of Christianity is similar to the lighted pictures of Jesus that were popular for a time: aglow but without a hint of humanness or life. Even the most fundamentalist misinterpretation of the Scriptures cannot erase the human dimension of a "crazy," stumbling movement led by, supported by, and sometimes defeated by real believing women and men.

No amount of ecstatic religious experience on that wonderful "first day" could change the accumulated human character of the original church assembly waiting for the Spirit in the upper room and the generations of assemblies to follow. Peter probably never really wanted to give up fishing or his wife. Against his will he ended up leading what was originally considered a schismatic movement within the Jewish synagogue, a movement designed by God to become Christianity. Not even visions (Acts 10:9–16) influenced Peter to stay on one side of a theological issue for long. Peter just tended to "Peter out." He did so when Jesus was arrested. He did so in Antioch when conservative Christians called the apostle Paul on the carpet. This is no putdown of Peter. This is who he was: a great man, a leader, and a minister—and human.

Wanting to climb the ladder to high places in church administration did not become an ecclesiastical temptation only in modern times. Zebedee's sons, James and John, tried it already with Jesus: "Teacher, we want you to do for us whatever we ask of you. . . . Grant us to sit, one at your right hand and one at your left, in your glory" (Mark 10:35ff).

They even got their mother to intercede for them for this chosen position in a kingdom that they presumed was going to be a powerful political thing (Matthew 20:20). Thomas did not start to doubt when news of resurrection spread. He probably was always the kind of person whose pattern was to insist: "Show me! Prove it!" He probably still tended to be that way a generation later as, according to tradition, he preached the gospel in India.

Philip wanted to see the Father, "and we will be satisfied" (John 14:8); and he, like the other apostles, never quite figured out eschatology.

Paul's missionary team couldn't get along with one another. If we read between the lines of Luke's idealized account of early church history, we glimpse these tensions and conflicts:

> . . . Paul said to Barnabas, "Come, let us return and visit the believers in every city where we proclaimed the word of the Lord and see how they are doing." Barnabas wanted to take with them John called Mark. But Paul decided not to take with them one who had deserted them in Pamphylia and had not accompanied them in the work. The disagreement became so sharp that they parted company (Acts 15:36ff).

The real cause of a split between Paul and Barnabas probably was the issue of eating with Gentile believers. (See Galatians 2:12–13.)

Paul was chased out of many towns both by Jews who believed in Jesus and by Jews who did not. This greatest of all apostles seemed to have had a knack of antagonizing people. He was beheaded for all his efforts. And who knows, he might have been in a foul mood the day he decided to limit the involvement of women.

It was a motley crew who broke the bread of remembering and shared the cup of unity. By human standards they were "losers" and quite possibly a little "crazy." Not all of them would have survived our interview process in parishes today! Why are they so special, then? And remembered today, two millennia later as great ministers of the gospel? With all of their humanness, they had experienced the presence of mystery among them, and responded to a call to ministry. They had experienced the Christ and were graced with the Spirit of God. This grace did not cancel out their humanity.

## Earthiness of Ministry

There has to be a human dimension to our ministry because, like Jesus, we are human, as are all the people we minister to. We might better use "earthiness" to describe this dimension of ministry. Our experiences, emotions, senses, intuition, and imagination are fueled with earthy images. The Catholic religion celebrates sacred mysteries with stories, symbols, with rituals that make use of material things. We find magic moments (in the sense of mystery) where we are most at home—on Earth.

ϒ

Attention to earthiness in our ministry is of critical importance to-day because we live in an age of high technology. Around the clock, the silicon chip provides experiences of learning, working, and en-tertainment never dreamed of in previous generations. While this offers its own opportunities for new kinds of religious experiences, more often than not it tends to remove real flesh and blood from our ministry. Saving relationships and loving actions will always be slower and more simple—of Earth. The more our culture moves us away from Earth, the more we need to make deliberate efforts to keep our feet on it, because it is here that our faith is incarnated.

Jesus ministered to flesh-and-blood people and revealed eternal mystery in very earthy ways. He touched bodies. He stayed solidly on Earth as he spun tales about seeds, weeds, fig trees, birds, sheep, goats, fish, yeast, vines, wine, splinters, employers and employees, and hospitality etiquette. People, in tune with Earth, listened and experienced mysteries of eternal truth.

Gospel characters, too, were very earthy: people with running sores and sightless eyes, quadraplegics, prostitutes, greedy tax gath-erers tired of cheating, religious leaders who thought they had all the answers, farmers frustrated with rocky fields, and fishers prob-ably tired of limited opportunity and surely tired of empty nets.

Scenes from his final real-life drama featured the best of earthy plots: bribery, betrayal, perjury, conviction, and execution—with the hero winning out in the end. His greatest act of ministry is his broken flesh and spilled blood.

The place and stuff of our ministry will always have this human, or earthy, dimension. Our responsibility will be to develop it, cel-ebrate it, and not ignore or avoid it. If our ministry is centered in the liturgy, we must develop a finely tuned appreciation of earthly ele-ments in ourselves and the people we serve: an appreciation of space, time, color, environment, the tension between light and dark, and of the momentum of seasons, the ebb and flow of sacramental objects, of bread, wine, oils, ashes, palm branches, flames, liturgical colors, of silence, song, and music, of a Word read and preached ef-fectively, of a spirit of greeting and hospitality.

If our ministry is centered in serving the needy, our time and ef-forts should not move far from the human and earthy because their needs are so human and earthy. We have to accept people un-conditionally in their real situation: hungry, homeless, sick, ter-minally ill, addicted, and mentally, physically, and emotionally handicapped. We have to hone the skills of listening and compassion, skills of locating and acquiring goods to be distributed to those in want, and skills of negotiating with secular and religious institutions. Many of the human skills and attitudes that are expected of care-giving professionals such as doctors, nurses, and psychotherapists are needed by women and men in helping ministries.

## The Light and Dark Sides of Ministers

Catholic experience through the ages should comfort us as we deal regularly with the mystery dimension and human dimension of our church and its many forms of ministry. Anyone who experiences a profound religious conversion, or walks with a friend through the RCIA process, knows that the human dimension remains intact. The wonder and even miracle of these experiences does not change the basic human nature, or Myers-Briggs profile, of people. In every group of ministers there will be extroverts and introverts, leaders and shy followers, decision makers and questioners, those who confuse and the confused. A minister's dysfunctional childhood is not erased when his or her vocation comes. A commitment to ministry radically changes neither the good nor the bad dynamics of a person. Ministers will be pretty much who they were before, unless some severe trauma or extensive therapy intervenes. Ministry may cater to the mystery dimension or the human dimension, but both will always be present.

Recognizing the human dimension of the church will help us to understand—though not condone—some of the great evils of the church. Some of these were shared by civil authorities, historically a powerful arm of the church in many countries. In the eleventh century, orders came from the highest offices in Rome to liquidate some French villages—men, women, and children—who were committed to the heresy of Albigensianism. Church officials ran the courts of the Inquisition, torturing and executing men and women accused of heresy.

Struggles with sexuality, attitudes toward women, hyper-attention to minute details of disciplinary rules binding under sin . . . the litany of human failures is endless.

Stories of people who "left" the church because of a bad experience with the humanity of their ministers are legion. There have been grouchy pastors, child-abusing staff members, dictatorial principals, insensitive confessors, and embezzling council members. There is the factual story of a pastor who kept the church doors locked, with a funeral procession waiting, until the local bank gave assurance that the dead person's check for belated "church dues" would clear. And the story of the pastor at communion during a funeral Mass who ordered the pall bearers to wheel the coffin out because the dead person had always left Mass at that time. And the pastors who risked death rather than keep their doors closed to the needy and who in fact were murdered.

Libraries of books on the church will be written; those who read them will gain new and deeper insights into the mystery of church. There will be workshops and popular renewal movements. The reality of the church, however, can be summed up by rephrasing the famous words of the cartoon character Pogo: "We have met the church and it is us!" A mixture of sin and grace, charismatic and institutional, virginal and sexual, cardinals and catechists, CCD sessions and ecumenical councils, Ku Klux Klan members and Mother Teresa, lean and fat, sober and drunk, ever newly born and yet wrinkled, giving hands and grasping. . . We've met the church and it's us. Thank God!

## Questions for Reflection and Discussion

1. Would you have been comfortable among the early ministers of Christianity? Why? Why not?

2. What is the most human element in ministry—good or bad— that you have experienced? Explain.

3. What human dynamic in _others_ are you most comfortable with? Most uncomfortable with?

4. What human dynamic in _yourself_ are you most comfortable with? Most uncomfortable with?

# — 8 —

# Ministering
# in a Catholic Church

### Religious Roots
An important part of the social nature of people is the human need
to be rooted in a clearly defined group of people such as a family,
tribe, clan, town, or nation. Associated with each of these divisions
of the human population is a highly developed and complicated
history of language, authority structures, traditions, taboos, laws—
and religion.

Most people are either born into or later initiated into a clearly
defined religious group with its particular interpretation of reality.
Sociologists call this interpretation of reality a plausibility structure.
It includes a definite set of convictions that cannot be compromised,
clearly identified leaders who define religious reality for adherents,
and a social process and rituals that help the group maintain its convictions and identity.

It is as difficult to separate ourselves from our religious roots as it
is to separate ourselves from other socially constructed groups such
as family, neighborhood, and ethnic ties. This is evident in taboos
regarding interracial marriages and guidelines for marriages involving mixed religions. Over the centuries, sanctions for violating
these taboos have ranged from raised eyebrows to death.

It is from one of these graced human groups, called the Catholic
church or parish, that ministry springs.

This experience of being rooted in a church is not an occasional
or transitional experience. People who share religious roots experience an identity with one another that is usually cultivated, pre-

served, and protected in some clearly defined group such as a parish. This is true even if they do not feel a particular affinity for one another on the basis of theological emphases or social status, or if they drift away from regular participation in the sacraments. These religious roots often originate with birth or even family location. Most people are eventually sealed in their religious roots by some public religious ritual such as baptism, conversion, dedication, confirmation, or bar mitzvah.

Some ministries that evolve in religious groups are designed to protect, explain, and pass on the group's religious roots by promoting traditions, rituals, and creeds. Disagreement with the group's religious authority or with its interpretation of faith creates tension, and people might even be accused of sin if they begin to examine the validity of their religious roots or inherited religious beliefs and traditions. Sometimes in history, such as during the inquisitions, death was the sentence for tampering with these religious roots.

## Catholic Roots

It is expected that women and men who are designated officially as ministers in a Catholic parish be rooted in the Catholic faith and actively participating in Catholic worship, sacraments, and other rituals. Although some may have recently received the sacraments of initiation, they now share these religious roots with all Catholics.

Not all commissioned ministers, however, need share the same theological attitudes and emphases. They may be conservative, liberal, or radical, but all are expected to be faithful Catholics. Catholic roots, though, should not be identified too narrowly, as if one particular "brand" of Catholicism has to stamp everyone in ministry. Such a narrowness is a curse to parishes and ministry teams. (See Chapter 9, Ministering in a Pluralistic Church.) One definition of "Catholic" is "open to all truth." Richard McBrien, well known for his synthesis of Catholicism, writes:

> . . . a more theologically fruitful approach to the question of Catholic distinctiveness would seem to lie in the direction of identifying and describing various characteristics of Catholicism, each of which Catholicism shared with one or another Christian church or tradition. But no other church or tradition possess these characteristics in quite the same way as Catholicism. In other words, there is particular *configuration* of char-

acteristics within Catholicism that is not duplicated anywhere else in the community of Christian churches. This configuration of characteristics is expressed in Catholicism's systematic theology; its body of doctrines; its liturgical life, especially the Eucharist; its variety of spiritualities; its religious congregations and lay apostolates; its official teachings on justice, peace, and human rights; its exercise of collegiality; and, to be sure, its Petrine ministry.

Catholicism is distinguished from other Christian churches and traditions especially in its understanding of, and practical commitment to, the principles of sacramentality, mediation, and communion. Differences between Catholic and non-Catholic (especially Protestant) approaches become clearer when measured according to these three principles *(Catholicism,* rev. ed.; see pages 9–16).

McBrien then summarizes these principles:

Sacramentality—"for Catholicism it is only in and through these material realities that we can encounter the invisible God."

Mediation—"Created realities not only contain, reflect, or embody the presence of God, they make that presence spiritually effective for those who avail themselves of these sacred realities."

Communion—"even when the divine-human encounter is most personal and individual, it is still communal, in that the encounter is made possible by the mediation of a community of faith."

Many parishioners, and some ministers, will insist that non-essentials in Catholic tradition are in fact essential. It is important, therefore, that a proper ordering of religious truths be adhered to and promoted. (See Chapter 16, When Theologies Clash.)

## Ecumenical Experiences

This Catholic identity founded on shared religious roots has to be reconciled occasionally with other experiences. Sometimes our faith crosses denominational lines in this ecumenical age. Consequently, we might find ourselves in closer *koinonia,* or spiritual union, with people from other denominations than we do with people from our own pews. We might even "feel church" more intensely with people from religious traditions other than with our own. This is especially true when our own sisters and brothers in faith do not seem to support our ministries and gospel convictions. Yet the Catholic experience continues to be very precious to us.

Being church is an historical, theological, and sociological phenomenon, but it is also a phenomenon involving the mysterious. To appreciate more deeply our calling to be both ecumenical and Catholic, it might help to speak of three moments of spiritual union that are more transitional than the dynamic of being rooted in a particular church. These are the moments of *bonding, assembling,* and *mission.*

The term "moment" is used here to describe what is often an intense but transitional experience of spiritual union. These are bits and pieces of time, relationships, and activities. A momentary experience of spiritual union is similar to that of friendship, love, sin, success, and failure. None of these is ever total in time, depth, or intensity; they are only moments along the continuum of the length, depth, and intensity of life.

This use of "moment" allows us to be comfortable with one particular institutional expression of church and religion—being religiously rooted as a Catholic—while at the same time experiencing spiritual union with persons outside our religious family. These transitional moments of spiritual union—bonding, assembling, and mission—also lie, of course, at the heart and foundation of the meaning of church. However, they can be isolated as dynamics related to, but outside of, established churches.

*Bonding*  A moment of religious bonding might be quite spontaneous, although many community-building efforts have bonding in mind. It occurs when two or more people experience a mystery of oneness, or communion. For a little while, a reality beyond ordinary human senses seems to cement several people into one people. This shared religious experience does not result in initiation into a particular organized faith community, but is a moment when two or more discover communion with each other that is somehow related to the wonderful mystery of God or the Christ.

People who enjoy a moment of bonding may or may not use identical terminology. Religious terminology usually belongs to patterns learned in family or organized formation efforts. Therefore, for a transitional moment a Catholic, Methodist, Orthodox, Jew, Buddhist, persons of no religious affiliation, and possibly persons who would consider themselves agnostics or atheists might experience a spiritual bonding. Shared terminology, on the other hand, does not guarantee religious bonding. Catholic pluralism proves this. Nor does different terminology prevent bonding. Ecumenical collaboration, worship, and service demonstrate this.

Jesus was firmly rooted in his Jewish traditions, holding membership in the synagogue at Capernaum and attending others. He shared these religious roots with most of the people he came in contact with. He shared them with close friends, such as Lazarus, Mary, and Martha of Bethany. Some of these contacts were very brief: some nighttime hours spent with Nicodemus, an intimate meal now and then with local families, such as with Zacchaeus in Jericho, and table fellowship with larger groups. He also shared religious roots with those who opposed his ministry. Jesus did not limit his bonding with these Jews, however. He enjoyed time with persons he did not share religious roots with. There were the Samaritan woman at Jacob's well, and the people in the crowds along the road, some of whom he healed, such as the daughter of the Syro-Phoenician woman. He features non-Jews favorably in his parable of the Good Samaritan and the healing of ten lepers.

*Assembling* This experience of bonding happens only if people come together. Thus, there is another kind of transitional experience of spiritual union outside one's own church: assembling, such as when we gather to share insights, prayer, or a celebration, or to plan and carry out service efforts. Assembling is a social dynamic that belongs to the very nature of being human. We are fully human only in relation to other people; we need to come together frequently because we are human.

The structures that give visibility to our transitional moments of assembling are not important in themselves. The important point is that they provide the opportunity for bonding. Assembly structures of established church communities have a kind of permanence, such as buildings and sanctuaries, rituals, books, and personnel. This is not the case with transitional assembling; nothing needs to continue beyond the actual coming together.

*Mission* Sometimes our social nature pulls us toward other human beings who are troubled, poor, sick, homeless, and ignored, hated. When our response to this pull happens outside our own established faith communities, we experience still another transitional moment of spiritual union, or communion. This is the moment of mission. Mission is not intended primarily to spread bonding ("getting more members," or proselytizing). It has to do, rather, with the very human, yet mysterious, matter of relating to and responding to human needs, working to eradicate what prevents people from being fully human.

In moments like these, even though we do not share religious roots, we become with others a saving people. Like Jesus, our purpose is not to expand our established faith communities, or to promote a religious cause, but rather to make people's human situation better. This mission to improve the lot of people is featured in Jesus' famous judgment scene parable (Matthew 25:31–42).

## Importance of Religious Roots and Ecumenism

These transitional and ecumenical moments of bonding, assembling, and mission are very important and further the reign of God. But they are not sufficient because we have to stay in touch with and relish our own religious roots. Otherwise we bring incomplete selves to transitional ecumenical activities, and confused selves to the ministry that springs from our own church.

People without clearly defined religious roots may even try to turn what is meant to be a transitional ecumenical moment into a permanently satisfying experience. This could very well violate the experience of others who are firmly rooted in a particular religious tradition but enjoying a transitional moment of union. Worse yet, the result may be to create a "church" that has no roots. This would be a contradiction and disastrous for ministry.

Our religious roots are with the parishioners we minister to and the leaders who give direction to our efforts, no matter how far from them we are in theological emphases and convictions.

## Questions for Reflection and Discussion

1. How firm are your Catholic roots? Describe a time you felt particularly happy that you are Catholic.

2. What are your fondest memories of ecumenical moments of bonding, assembling, and mission? How do these compare with your ordinary Catholic experiences?

3. Does your parish have good relations with non-Catholic religious groups? Why? Why not?

# — 9 —

# Ministering
# in a Pluralistic Church

## Practice vs Theory

Religious reality for one person is not necessarily the same for another, even in the same parish or on the same parish team. A fact of human life is that people relate to sacred mysteries in at least slightly different ways. Ever since Pentecost there has been a tension between how the church wants its baptized members to believe and how they actually understand and live their faith—a tension between theory and practice. Continuing reflection on the part of theologians, church leaders, and individual believers results in religious *theory*. What should God's community of the baptized be like?

The actual *practice* of faith challenges the orderly content of theological theory. Practical faith evolves from one's personality and immediate experience, from the charism of a preacher, the influence of significant others, from a particular emphasis—or bias—in faith formation, cultural factors, and the need of people to live religiously in practical and personal ways. Often this leads to a preoccupation with a particular religious reality or interpretation of religious reality, with an intensely behavioral dimension: a functioning religious identity. (See Chapter 11, Clarifying Our Religious Identity.) A normal consequence is a pluralism within a religious group such as a parish.

The Catholic church has always been complex and pluralistic. Post-Vatican II parishes did not invent the pluralism we observe today.

The New Testament (NT) gives indications of very diverse views within Christianity as well as references to Christian groups regarded as radically deviant by NT writers. Sometimes the views are espoused by different groups co-existing within the same city as, for instance, the four affiliations described in I Corinthians 1:12 or the dispute at Antioch (Galatians 2:12–14). Sometimes one form of Christian outlook may have been prominent in one area and another in a different area, as we can deduce from comparing very different NT works that show no knowledge of each other. Nevertheless, the image of a totally homogeneous Christianity in the first Christian century is hard to erase.

With these words alluding to pluralism in the first generation of Christianity, Raymond E. Brown and John P. Meier begin their book, _Antioch & Rome_ (p. vii). If it is hard, as they maintain, to erase the image of a totally homogeneous _first-century_ Christianity, it is even harder, for many if not most Catholics, to erase the image of a totally homogeneous church life for the past nineteen centuries. How the church functioned in their youth or in the time of their immediate ancestors is presumed by some Catholics to be the way the church functioned at the time of the apostles. In theory, there may be one Catholic faith. In practice, however, there has never been in the Catholic church one way of believing or one way of practicing what is believed. On the functional level, no one particular expression of faith, of an individual or of an organized group, gives an adequate account of the significance and content of believing, or of motives for believing.

## Benefits of Pluralism

The Extraordinary Synod of Bishops in Rome in 1985 admitted the benefits of positive pluralism in the church. What they said about the unity and pluriformity of particular churches (parishes, dioceses, national conferences) within the universal Catholic church can be applied to the pluralism within the local parish: "When pluriformity is true richness and carries with it fullness, this is true catholicity. The pluralism of fundamentally opposed positions instead leads to dissolution, destruction, and the loss of identity" (_A Message to the People of God and the Final Report_, p. 18). Archbishop Pio Laghi, the Apostolic Pronuncio to the U.S., echoed this same theme with even stronger words while speaking to the U.S. bishops at their 1987 fall conference: "A plurality that cannot be integrated into unity is chaos; unity unrelated to plurality is tyranny."

It is a function of ministry to make a pluralistic expression of faith possible in a parish, rather than impossible:

> In community we find our individual biases and convictions bounded by, complemented by, and challenged by others. This is both a threat and a gift. As a gift my community—indeed my religious tradition—fills out the narrowness of my own vision, welcomes my strengths and special insights, and makes up for my limitations. Pluralism, in this understanding, is an essential characteristic of a believing community, not to be apologized for, denied, or simply overcome, but to be invoked as a resource and strength. This is how faith flourishes in a group and carries individual belief beyond itself; this is how we are incorporated and our faith made communal" (Whitehead, *Community of Faith,* p. 9).

## Transition to a New Pluralism

While it is true that there has always been a plurality of ways of living Catholic faith, our current pluralism has features absent in previous generations. Until recent years there was a shared religious identity among Catholics of the Latin Roman Catholic church locally and worldwide that created a unity bordering on uniformity. This is no longer true. Since the 1960s, Catholics, even in the same parish, have gone from the comforts of a shared Catholic identity to a new and, for many, an uncomfortable pluralism. Different religious convictions and practices *without the previous common meaning or obvious Catholic identity holding all together* are evident. It is a pluralism that can be described with words unheard of before Vatican II: anger, aggression, stress, conflict, judgment, polarization, confrontation, etc. These emotions are understandable. For a long time, centuries in fact, faith had been identified with a conventional Catholicism founded on similar theology manuals, catechisms, and sermons throughout the nation and even throughout the world.

The passing of this popular Catholic identity before a new identity could evolve was traumatic for many parishioners. Some aggressively held on to what had been precious to them in the pre-Vatican II conventional Catholicism, even if the official church no longer stressed it and the local parish no longer supported it. Others answered a call to deeper insights into the meaning of church and ministries. The latter became committed to important new movements founded upon experience and gospel, even if the parish or the church at large did not concur. In some parishes, religious groups began functioning separately from each other and some even separately from the parish itself. A sense of unity, once lacking between the Catholic church and other religions, now seemed lacking among Catholics themselves.

## Breaking Apart?

As we approach the third millennium, this pluralism among Catholics is not centered primarily in liturgical matters: how we worship and celebrate the sacraments. It is centered more in matters of discipline in the Catholic tradition, along with social, political, and moral issues on the American scene. Catholics are vocal on both sides of the abortion and other pro life issues; on both sides of the issue of the use of authority in the church; on both sides of the question of the ordination of women and married men; on both sides of United States military and foreign policies; even on both sides of racial and discrimination issues.

Conflicts can become so heated that a final split within the Catholic church might seem possible:

> . . . the real question facing the church today . . . is the unaskable one, perhaps. The question that really needs to be answered is not, "Which of these groups is right?" In a time of massive social, scientific and political change, there is more than enough truth, more than enough confusion to go around on each of these apparently separate sides. . . .The real question is whether or not the Catholic church is in a state of veritable schism. Has the church split wide open, beyond repair, and no one is saying so because to say it is to admit that it has happened? (Chittister, *National Catholic Reporter,* January 28, 1994)

Then Chittister puts a positive spin on the troubled features of pluralism among Catholics:

> I am convinced that rather than being in a state of schism, the church has perhaps never for centuries shown more restraint or more unity than it is showing now. . . .Because whatever the amount of confusion, whatever the pressure, whatever the ten-

sions within the church as well as outside of it, the church, with a long sense of history and total disregard for time, has with a few tragic exceptions managed to avoid the temptation to revert to wholesale condemnations and inquisitions and indices.

## Sectarian Tendencies

The positive values of pluralism should not excuse tendencies to crawl off into a corner and turn one's back on other Catholics. While schism may be avoided, there is still the sin of sectarianism. Seldom has this sociological dynamic been used to describe situations within Catholicism. Our strong traditional central authority has prevented sectarian tendencies in the past. The term "sect" is used in Protestant tradition to describe a group that breaks away from an established church. Brown briefly considers the notion of sectarianism in studying the pluralistic character of the early church and specifically the Johannine Christians who gave birth to the fourth gospel (*The Community of the Beloved Disciple*, pp. 14ff). However, taking "sectarian" in a strictly religious context, he argues that it does not apply because the religious group, the Johannine Christians, did not break communion (*koinonia*) with other Christians.

Sectarianism can be examined as a sociological phenomenon, which does not necessarily preclude a total break between groups of parishioners or between these groups and the rest of the church community. Understanding the dynamics of sectarianism becomes very helpful, then, in appreciating what is happening in today's parishes and its effect on ministry.

> The term "sect" is used in different ways in common speech. Sociologically, it means a religious group that is relatively small, in tension with the larger society and closed (one might say "balled up") against it and that makes very strong claims on the loyalty and solidarity of its members. The choice to persist in defiant cognitive deviance necessarily also entails the choice of social organization (Berger, *Rumor of Angels*, p. 23).

This definition of "sect" accurately describes the lived experience of parish teams who minister in the midst of Catholics United for the Faith, charismatics, Bayside devotees, and the many other conservative and progressive groups functioning in the parish. The groups are "relatively small" in relation to the parish as a whole. They are often "in tension with the larger society" of the parish, causing and experiencing stress and sometimes suspicion and conflict. Such groups become "closed against" the parish when the parish threatens their legitimacy by refusing to support their claims and agenda or by denying them any legitimacy.

One of the dynamics of sects is that adherents turn to one another, creating a social organization or closed group high on loyalty and solidarity, legitimating for one another their interpretation of religious reality. An attitude of "we against them" and "we're right, you're wrong" is expressed in public statements and behavior. A spirit of elitism and separatism solidifies group members, even though most will continue to participate in essential parish activities, including the weekend liturgy, walking to the communion table with other parishioners. However, it is not unheard of that groups will protest some policy or practice on the church steps.

Another sociological dynamic of sectarianism, "cognitive deviance," offers still another insight into the pluralistic tendencies in Catholic parishes today. "Cognitive deviance" is the choice a group makes because it fears certain trends. It is a deliberate choice not to follow the crowd but to go their own way and to legitimize this choice by

[huddling] together with like-minded deviants—and huddle very closely indeed. Only in a counter-community of considerable strength does cognitive deviance have a chance to maintain itself. The counter-community provides continuing therapy against the creeping doubt as to whether, after all, one may not be wrong and the majority right. To fulfill its function of providing social support for the deviant body of "knowledge," the counter-community must provide a strong sense of solidarity among its members. . . .In sum, it must be a kind of ghetto (Berger, p. 22).

Reflecting on these words, it is easy to think of the brief history of some of the groups functioning in and perhaps in spite of the Catholic parish today. If the "deviant" group is relatively small, we might tend to write the members off as fanatics. However, if it is a "counter-community of considerable strength," either in size or influence, then an altogether different parish dynamic is involved and parish ministers must adequately meet the challenge.

The nature of a sect is to have a definite set of convictions that cannot be compromised, a clearly identified leader who defines reality for adherents, and a process that helps the sect maintain its convictions and itself as a group. This is called a "plausibility structure." All religious groups, including those with sectarian tendencies, need this kind of structure. For the latter, seldom is the identified leader an official of the Catholic church. In fact, it is not uncommon that groups both on the "left" and on the "right" will speak out against the pastor, the bishop, or even the pope. New "reality-definers"—part of every plausibility structure—have appeared on the scene. These might be a theologian such as Hans Küng or a relatively unknown person claiming to see visions and receive divine messages. They can be helpful members of a parish pastoral team or a thorn in its side.

While some individuals have left the parish because of these sectarian tendencies, the parish team still has an opportunity—a ministry—to come to grips with divergent groups because the parish is still *home* to most of them, and because sectarian tendencies will more likely increase than go away. (See Chapters 16, When Theologies Clash, and 17, Adapting to Change.)


## Questions for Reflection and Discussion

1. How closely does your practical faith match the theoretical Catholic family?

2. Are you more comfortable with the stability of uniformity of belief or the freedom and instability of pluralism? Explain.

3. What negative features of pluralism have you personally experienced?

4. What groups in your parish show sectarian tendencies? Does your own group of significant others? If so, describe them.

# — 10 —

# Ministering
# as Leaders

## New Times in the Catholic Church

"Church is a very simple structure. It only gets complicated when
you involve people in it!"

"But that's what church is—'people' is what we're about!"

This simple exchange between a diocesan office director and a
bishop pretty well summarizes the paradox of both the simplicity
and complexity of church life today. On the one hand, our ministry
makes us instruments of the reign of God, making visible God's
powerful and loving presence. On the other hand, we have to accomplish this within and through human structures. This was true
from the beginning of Christianity.

Leadership in the local community affects ministry in two ways.
First, an important form of lay ministry is that of shared leadership
in the local parish. Second, all parish ministries are affected in some
way by these leadership groups that promote, initiate, supervise,
and evaluate parish activities.

We know little of the exact structures of early Christian communities. They seemed to have continued patterns of leadership
and coordination that served them well within their Jewish experience and while they maintained contact with synagogues. After
a final separation from the synagogues, three key ministries continued and are evident in the letters to the churches and in Acts of
the Apostles. *Teachers* and *prophets* were common in Jewish synagogue life. The same ministry on the part of Christian teachers and
prophets was popular among the followers of the new way of Jesus.
They encouraged believers and applied the words and stories of
Jesus to current issues. These teachers and prophets were naturally

part of the leadership in the communities because they handed on what the community had come to believe. Through their ministry the followers of the new way "devoted themselves to the apostles' teaching" (Acts 2:42). They presided over the Eucharist in many places.

Another pattern of religious leadership was exercised by the *elders* of the church community. This leadership structure was common in the civil/secular world of New Testament times and had been adopted by most synagogues. In the Greek language elders were called *presbyteroi* ("presbyters"), a ministry of leadership that would evolve in the second century into a priesthood. Elders in the Jerusalem synagogues featured prominently in the suffering and death of Jesus and in the early persecution of his followers. This pattern of leadership, however, was such a normal part of their religious experience that Christian Jews carried it over into their own communities.

Paul seemed to have preferred a leadership exercised by teachers and prophets. However, he is described in Acts as appointing elders to lead the local communities of faith that he founded through preaching or visited on his evangelizing journeys: "And after they had appointed elders for them in each church, with prayer and fasting they entrusted them to the Lord in whom they had come to believe" (Acts 14:23). "From Miletus he sent a message to Ephesus, asking the elders of the church to meet him. When they came to him, he said to them: '. . . Keep watch over yourselves and over all the flock, of which the Holy Spirit has made you overseers, to shepherd the church of God that he obtained with the blood of his own Son . . .'" (Acts 20:17ff).

Letters to the churches also presume that elders were in charge of the community: "Now as an elder myself and a witness of the sufferings of Christ, as well as one who shares in the glory to be revealed, I exhort the elders among you to tend the flock of God that is in your charge, exercising the oversight, not under compulsion but willingly, as God would have you do it—not for sordid gain but eagerly. Do not lord it over those in your charge, but be examples to the flock" (1 Peter 5:1ff). "Are any of you sick? They should call for the elders of the church and have them pray over them. . ." (James 5:13ff).

It seems that these groups of elders looked to one among them as *chief elder*. In the second and third centuries this chief elder evolved into bishop-priest-pastor, and the assistant elders into priest-pastors. Sharing in this ministry of leadership were deacons.

While the language used to describe these groups of elders sounds strange to contemporary Catholic ears, the pattern itself should not. These bodies of elders would be the equivalent of our diocesan and parish councils, commissions, committees, with the chief elder being our diocesan bishop or parish pastor.

## Church Structures and Processes Today

The church today is still a local gathering of disciples who have chosen through baptism to follow the way of Jesus. Some in the local church, as in all the ancient centers of Christianity, are called to the ministry of leadership. Vatican II called for lay persons to offer their advice and prudent counsel to pastors. Soon parish councils and a system of committees were developed in parishes with varying degrees of success. In 1983, Canon 129 of the Code of Canon Law assigned this ministry of leadership first of all to the ordained clergy assigned to the parish by the bishop, and secondly to lay persons:

1. In accord with the prescriptions of law, those who have received sacred orders are capable of the power of governance, which exists in the Church by divine institution and is also called the power of jurisdiction.

2. Lay members of the Christian faithful can cooperate in the exercise of this power in accord with the norm of law.

Canons 511 and 512 describe their leadership on the diocesan level:

In each diocese, to the extent that pastoral circumstances recommend it, a pastoral council is to be established whose responsibility it is to investigate under the authority of the bishop all those things which pertain to pastoral works, to ponder them and to propose practical conclusions about them.

The pastoral council consists of Christian faithful who are in full communion with the Catholic church, clerics, members of institutes of consecrated life and especially lay persons, who are designated in a manner determined by the diocesan bishop.

Canon 536 established a similar leadership role for the laity on the parish level:

After the diocesan bishop has listened to the presbyteral council and if he judges it opportune, a pastoral council is to be established in each parish; the pastor presides over it, and
through it the Christian faithful along with those who share in
the pastoral care of the parish in virtue of their office give their
help in fostering pastoral activity.

In the Catholic church in the United States there was a tendency
to create a political model based on secular experience, using a system of nomination and election and meeting procedures based on
that experience, looking to these new forms of leadership as ad-
visory or governing boards of directors. It became common for constitutions and by-laws to be drawn up that called for titles such as
President and Vice President. Each member had a vote, and the pastor had veto authority. A pastor's veto could be appealed to a higher level, to a vicar in a vicariate system, a dean in a deanery system,
or to the bishop himself.

These new patterns in Catholic parishes invited greater involvement from parishioners in the ministry of leadership. Not sur-
prisingly, they also created numerous problems associated with
political structures in general and church structure in particular.
Obstacles to effective ministry were often a consequence.

The problems associated with leadership structures—councils,
committees—are connected with one or more of three categories:
people, education, and structure. Since it is important to identify accurately the source of the problem, we must ask: Is it in the structure itself—in the constitution and by-laws, or operating
procedures? Is the problem caused by one or more persons who understand the structure, but who choose not to cooperate with the
structure or with the other people? Is there ignorance of roles, responsibilities, or relationships?

The actual source of a problem in one of these leadership groups
might be so subtle that it is hard to identify. For example, someone
might question whether a parishioner who is paid for part-time
ministry be allowed to serve on a parish council as an elected or selected member at large. The chairperson might identify the problem
as structural and seek clarification from a higher governing body,
such as the diocese. But the problem might not be structural at all; it
might have to do with persons and personalities. There might be a
reason why some council members do not want a particular individual to serve with them. Instead of dealing with the actual "people

problem," they seek a solution in structure—diocesan guidelines.

Neither parish nor diocesan guidelines can anticipate every possible problem, so it is important to analyze the situation carefully and then focus on the real problem before attempting to solve it through structural changes.

Another example: If the education committee decides that a light should be installed in a certain location, may the pastor on his own authority have it installed someplace else? Or must he go through an administration committee? While this sounds minor, further questioning might reveal that the real problem is not where the light should be placed and who should make the decision about it, but rather a pattern of conflict between a pastor and parish committees. Are individuals on committees trying to take over the pastor's authority and operate as a governing board of directors? Is the pastor resisting this with contrary unilateral decisions?

The point of this illustration is that at first glance the problem appears to be a people problem: The pastor has an autocratic style and does not work well with committees. However, the problem might be educational. The committees might not understand their authority and role in relation to that of the pastor. It is a people problem if the committees do understand their proper role and the pastor's but some members do not accept this relationship of roles. They choose instead to create a power conflict.

Educational problems should be solved by informing committee members about the basics of the structure, roles, and relationships, operating procedures, etc., as defined in constitutions and by-laws of parish or diocesan guidelines.

People problems should be solved through conflict management techniques, including use of an outside facilitator if needed. (See these sections in Chapter 16: "Principles of Conflict Resolution," and "Theological Reflection and Conflict Resolution.")

Structural problems should be resolved by revising guidelines, constitutions, and by-laws.

## Shared Goals and Perspectives

Parishioners who share in the leadership ministry in local parishes should also be committed to shared parish goals. (See Chapter 24, Tapping into God's Dream.) Work on shared goals produces a sense of ownership. This in turn increases interest, pride, and participation in the parish community. Community spirit, an _esprit de corps_, grows as individuals come to know and enjoy one another in parish leadership groups. Friendships are formed and nourished in frequent meetings.

Parish leadership groups can accomplish wonderful things when members work together in a harmonious and productive way, motivated by the spirit of the gospels and the good of the parish community. A variety of viewpoints, experiences, gifts, and practiced skills of individual ministers, when tapped as fully as possible, produce synergy—a working together. This will create goals, solve problems, and do the kind of effective ministry that no individual, even the most hard-working and gifted individual with extensive credentials, can accomplish alone. This is a primary benefit of groups that work well together.

Synergy flows out of the relationship the ministers have to one another. The very stuff that generates this potentially exciting synergy, however, may cause some to stumble and withdraw into themselves. This happens when one or other parish minister, lay or ordained, is uncomfortable with one or more of these relationships. Will they function well when there is a coming together of male and female? Of young and old? Of lay and ordained? Of different theologies? Of different personality types? Of different social standings and emotional temperaments?

This principle of synergy should also flow out of the relationship of ministers to the parishioners they serve. Parishioners' perspectives on various topics and situations may be very different from those of the parish team. To serve the parish well, it is important that parish leaders listen to these differences, and even seek to learn what they are. This sharing of perspectives creates a joint effort that leads to creative approaches and solutions to problems and challenges. It is an easy but important way for pastors and parish teams to keep in touch with the worldview of the parishioners. It is equally important to respect differences in perspectives, which may create a healthy tension in the parish community. To be aware of differences but dismiss them as simply uninformed or unimportant can create unhealthy tension. This prevents or interferes with achieving goals and effective problem-solving. It also creates a negative environment, a bad spirit in the parish.

## Positive Environment

It is critically important to be well aware of the particular culture, profile, and style of the parish community one is serving. One parish may be composed primarily of parishioners who work in the professions at a fairly high level, with many business and professional skills. Another parish may be primarily a blue collar or rural community. Some parishes may be ethnically homogeneous, while others may be quite diverse. Some parishes may serve a retirement community; others may serve primarily young families.

The different culture, profile, and style of parish or the many different styles within a parish naturally determine the style of meetings held: procedures used, time scheduled, degree of formality, etc. The way the parish organizes its ministries, structures, and manner of operating in order to minister effectively must reflect the mix of people and the cultures and values they bring with them. _One size does not fit all._

A function of the ministry of leadership, then, is to create a positive environment in which all members of the parish function to the best of their ability. Negative behavioral patterns of relating to others need to be redirected so that a creative, joyful, and compassionate spirit can replace the negativity and cynicism that are so common. Parishes have a marvelous opportunity to become places where people can experience the joy of a Christian community that respects differences and celebrates the gifts each member brings to the whole. Parishes can be places where diversity is valued as a strength rather than seen as an obstacle. (See Chapter 9, Ministering in a Pluralistic Church.)

In order to create this positive environment for ministry, parish leadership must learn the skills necessary to coordinate group efforts effectively. These skills are not always self-evident but can be acquired if parish ministers see them as important. They can be learned as any skill is learned: through practice. Special skills are necessary to interact with difficult persons or to resolve interpersonal problems that arise within a leadership group. The more we grow in this particular area of ministry, the more effectively we will carry out our ministry of leadership.

## Questions for Reflection and Discussion

1. How clearly defined is the ministry of leadership in your parish? Does it tend to be democratic? Autocratic? Does it have vision? Direction?

2. Has the leadership ministry in your parish experienced problems? If so, do you feel that the source of the problem was correctly identified and dealt with?

3. Do you feel that the leaders in your parish have a good grasp of parish goals? Explain.

4. Are those in leadership positions in your parish open to the insights of rank and file parishioners? If so, give examples. If not, why not?

# — 11 —

# Clarifying Our
# Religious Identity

## Description of Religious Identity

In Chapter 9 we saw that from the beginning pluralism in the Catholic church has been more the norm than the exception. There is always a tension between theory and practice in the mystery of faith. Another way to understand practical faith is to see it as a *functioning* religious identity. All of us have one. We are not Catholic in some theoretical fashion. Our faith has skin on it, so to speak.

A functioning religious identity provides a structure by which our faith, religious convictions, and religious practices hold together, make sense, and are ritualized. It provides us with spiritual security, including the ultimate security of eternal salvation. This is why most people will not permit their religious convictions and traditions to be challenged, ridiculed, or in any way tampered with. Their religious security—and comfort—is threatened.

A religious identity, therefore, describes who a person *actually* is, religiously. It describes a behavioral and oftentimes intense dimension of a person's religious life. It influences how we pray, how we feel about God, how we view the church, what kind of moral decisions we make, how we want others to believe and behave, and how we minister to others.

## Evolution of Religious Identity

Religious identity is as much a sociological phenomenon as a theological one. It evolves, therefore, like any other feature of our human personality. It is gradually constructed by those who most influence us: family, friends, teachers, and church leaders such as pastors and catechists. Words are spoken, prayers are said, rituals are performed, traditions are carried out, and in this way a particular complex of religious ideas are fostered, maintained, and accepted as real by children and adult catechumens.

Few of us were responsible originally for constructing our religious identity. We grew into it during the earliest years of our experience. It took shape, first of all, from what we heard, saw, and felt as infants and young children in our homes. There were popular prayer forms used at table, bed time, and possibly some private devotions. Older parishioners among us were influenced by the many religious practices associated with sacramentals such as medals, scapulars, holy water, and the holy pictures on the walls of homes and schools.

Our religious identity continued to evolve when we were old enough to participate in church functions. Preaching, singing hymns, public devotions, and formal religious education sessions molded our religious reality in unashamedly deliberate ways. Even the statues, the stations of the cross on the church walls, and the stained-glass windows subtly influenced how we felt about ourselves religiously.

The religious reality and images that resulted from this formation did not have to be logical or even make sense. The same is true today, and especially of children. What is important to the children is that they use the religious words and do the religious things that appear important to the adults around them.

The curriculum used in a formation process is a main source of religious identity. From the late 1800s until the early 1960s this was the Baltimore Catechism for most Catholics in the United States. The widespread use of this one source and method of religious formation resulted in a uniform religious identity shared by most Catholics. This shared religious identity fragmented in the 1960s and 1970s as the church moved into the first phases of reform and renewal. New curricula and new forms of catechesis then became popular.

Our early childhood religious experiences are a very important part of our story, but they are only the beginning. Continuing faith formation opportunities and religious experiences gradually add to, clarify, correct, or replace what originally just rubbed off on us or was deliberately planted in us in our youth. Unless we invest ourselves personally in some form of continuing faith formation process, we might very well drift through life with the immature or even incorrect notions of childhood. At the same time, we should take care that not too many new religious notions come crowding in so quickly that we no longer know who we are religiously and are no longer secure in our religious identity.

## Importance of Clarifying Religious Identity

Our functioning religious identity is of critical importance if we are commissioned as lay ministers. In a very real sense, who we are is just as important as what we say or do in our ministry. In fact, probably more so. We want to share with others who we have become because of our own religious history. The First Letter of John (1:1–4) focuses on this:

> We declare to you what was from the beginning, what we have heard, what we have seen with our eyes, what we have looked at and touched with our hands . . . so that you also may have fellowship with us. . . so that our joy may be complete.

We have a tendency to promote our own religious insights and attitudes, doctrinal convictions and biases, what we see as priorities in the gospel and in traditional religious teaching, how we understand the meaning of church, how we view ministry, and what our favorite religious traditions are. Even if we do not actively promote these, they still influence our ministry very much. Put simply, how we understand the mystery of God and how we relate to God rubs off on those we minister to.

It is very important, therefore, that we have a clear sense of our functioning religious identity. We do not come by this easily today. In fact, a confused religious identity is probably more common than a finely tuned one. In the less volatile times before Vatican II, we might more readily have known who we were in a religious sense. In those times we could easily tell when we or others deviated, even in the slightest degree, from the conventional Catholic pattern. That is no longer true because of the transitions that have taken place in our contemporary church. Reform movements continue. Comfortable features of that older and more clearly defined religious identity have passed away. Religious pluralism is widespread. Our experiences of a variety of adult faith formation opportunities have resulted in new religious insights and modifications of our original religious identity.

The result can be "option shock" in religious matters. There are so many new insights, new choices, different religious emphases that we may no longer have a clear understanding, in a religious sense, of who we are or who we are called to be. With so many options available, we may avoid making any choice at all!

A second effect of "option shock" is the temptation to play "follow the leader" or "Simon says." This is a lazy way out of the quandary, basing one's religious identity and spirituality, without serious reflection, upon the most recent popular religious resource or new form of adult formation, or spiritual guru. The consequence is religious drift. We avoid coming to grips with core issues in life and faith and consequently cannot be an effective spiritual guide for others.

### Religious Identity in Times of Transitions

Clarifying our religious identity is particularly important for those who have experienced a transition from an older, more conventional form of Catholicism. Following the Council of Trent (1545-1563), the church entered an era that gave the impression of a *finished condition*. We knew what the church was, we defined it in precisely worded decrees (and anathemas), and went about being that church for four hundred years. It took another council, Vatican II, with its carefully worded decrees (no anathemas this time), to remind us that the carefully defined church of the 1500s-1900s needed reform, renewal, and change. *Ecclesia semper reformanda:* The church would always be in need of reform. It is not in finished form yet.

Then, in less than a generation, that same old temptation tends to creep in: We now know what the church is! We want it to be made in our own image. If it reflects our own current convictions, then all is well—and the church's formation is finished!

Nothing that comes into being is permanent. Nothing that has a human dimension is changeless; neither what is living nor what we construct. We can learn a powerful lesson from an old, abandoned house. Sometimes all that remain are foundation stones and some parts of walls. Even if these have disappeared, there remains evidence of a house of long ago. In rural areas this might be an evergreen tree deliberately planted once for shade and now standing out of line with trees on the horizon, drooping lilac bushes now just wood, and perhaps some fruit trees long barren but once part of an orchard.

This need not be a sad scene, because it reflects a deeper reality.

Generations of life once filled this house: the excitement of new beginnings and the ever-repeating cycle of promise in weddings, love-making, births, childhood games, sickness, deaths, success, and failure. There is an identity between the house and the people who had lived there. Now, long abandoned by descendants of people who knew it as home, people walk past the shell of a house without a thought, and the descendants of those who lived there find life elsewhere.

Historical transitions happen in all things that come into being. There is a cycle of birth, life, death—and always promise of new life. The first six chapters in this book explored major historical transitions that have happened and are still happening in the Catholic church and the ministries that continue to bring about God's reign of saving power and love. There is a passing of some forms of religious identities and ministries as people go about living church today. We cannot live today's church in the absolute forms of yesterday. The church, too, lives an ever-repeating cycle of birth, life, death—and new life. This is the church's destiny. And ours.

It is understandable that parishioners—and even leaders at the highest levels—feel threatened and agonize over the passing of their church as they knew it. Within that church they were conceived. In the faithful practice of their religion they experienced spiritual security. Their Catholic religion brought laughter and love, but also tears and fears. Like their ancestors before them, people expected to grow old in this church, clutching to themselves the memories of all that had made so much sense. Then it seems that almost overnight their children, friends, and even, they suspected, the church itself abandoned the beliefs and practices that had given them so much meaning. Their comfortable church, like an abandoned house, fell, and people walked past it, almost in a hurry to build a new church.

## Humility with New Movements and Transitions

It is important, then, that we not find our religious identity so closely attached to a particular religious movement or a particular form of ministry that we cannot adjust to new times. New religious movements are ever evolving in the church, and new and popular religious traditions and identities gradually replace the old. These cycles, always present in the church, must and will go on.

Forms of ministry, too, have a cycle of birth, life, death—and new life, as we saw in Chapters 1-6. Like the church community, this cycle does not end at any one time in history. Therefore, even we who come to faith and ministry at this exciting time in history need humility. Our "new" religious viewpoints and efforts that we devote ministerial energy to will not always be new, and people will walk past them one day, too. We have not arrived at the finished condition!

If the church were finished soon after Pentecost, we would still belong to synagogues. If the church were finished during the age of the apostles, we would be worshiping in Greek and would not know a eucharistic priesthood. If the church were finished at the time of great monasteries, we would be ministered to by monks who would return to their walled homes at dusk. If the church were finished before it reached the north countries, we would not know Christmas trees and Advent wreaths.

If the church were finished before the Reformation, we would have some popes and bishops buying and selling lucrative chunks of church influence and real estate. And if the church were finished in 1950, we would not know of frequent communion, nor would we have enjoyed the eucharist as a sacred meal, nor have reached out and taken the bread the Lord asked us to take, nor have the laity proclaiming the Word to congregations.

If the church were finished, if ministry had achieved its final and most perfect, most effective forms—the final coming of Christ would happen. Most of us suspect that much more change will take place before that moment arrives. (See Chapter 17, Adapting to Change.)

The chapters that follow give further direction in this clarification of our functioning religious identity. (Also, see Chapter 8, Ministering in a Catholic Church.)

## Questions for Reflection and Discussion

1. What do you cherish most about the religious identity you had 10–20 years ago? Do you ever revert to it? Under what circumstances? What do you cherish most about the religious identity you now have?

2. Which features of contemporary Catholicism confuse you? Make you uncomfortable? Excite you? How do you think your answers match those of other lay ministers?

3. Who was most influential in the early formation of your func-

tioning religious identity? How did this happen? Who has been most influential in changes in your religious identity since your childhood? How did this happen? How do you feel about having the same kind of influence on those to whom you minister?

4. Are any basic elements of Catholicism particularly weak in your patterns of behavior and belief? If so, describe them.

5. What forms of ministry do you suspect will evolve further? Should die? Should last until the final coming?

6. How would you feel if your current ministry were replaced by other forms?

PART THREE

Responding
Maturely
to Challenges

# — 12 —

# Developing Confidence as a Minister

## Tension Between Vocation and Confidence

Strange! Being called by the Lord to ministry often takes the form of having one's arm twisted by the pastor or other member of the parish team. Regardless of how the call comes, few of us have the confidence that Isaiah the prophet had: "Then I heard the voice of the Lord saying, 'Whom should I send and who will go for us?' And I said, 'Here I am, send me!'" (Isaiah 6:8) Or the quickness with which apostles dropped everything and followed Jesus:

> As Jesus passed along the Sea of Galilee, he saw Simon and his brother Andrew casting a net into the sea—for they were fishermen. And Jesus said to them, "Follow me and I will make you fish for people." And immediately they left their nets and followed him. As he went a little farther, he saw James son of Zebedee and his brother John, who were in their boat mending the nets. Immediately he called them; and they left their father Zebedee in the boat with the hired men, and followed him (Mark 1:16–20).

We are in good company if we feel inadequate at times. Moses, too, had this feeling, even though he had extraordinary experiences to fall back on, including a divine voice speaking out of a burning bush and the example of his staff that became a snake. He tried to slip away from the Lord's call with the plea that he was inadequate: "O my Lord, I have never been eloquent, neither in the past nor

---

even now that you have spoken to your servant; but I am slow of speech and slow of tongue" (Exodus 4:10,13).

Jeremiah tried the same tactic. "Ah, Lord God! Truly I do not know how to speak, for I am only a boy" (Jeremiah 1:6). Only with Moses did God negotiate, allowing him to slip out of a portion of his assignment: "What of your brother Aaron, the Levite? I know that he can speak fluently. . . . You shall speak to him and put the words in his mouth; and I will be with your mouth and with his mouth, and will teach you what you shall do" (Exodus 4:14–15).

We have every reason to be confident that God's call to us, however it happened in the concrete, comes with the necessary gifts for ministry. We are no longer helpless babies and children. Over the years we have grown into mature, talented, educated, experienced women and men. But when faced with unfamiliar tasks, or ones we are not doing well with, we can become as helpless as a child again. This is understandable, because failure and new situations are not pleasant experiences. They may be challenging, yes, but they certainly are not comfortable. We need not, then, be ashamed of occasional feelings of inadequacy.

While parishes do set up required credentials for certain designated ministries, there is no one particular talent or personality trait required of most. Desire alone, though, is not enough. It is not unusual for a parish to have some willing, enthusiastic but quite ineffective ministers. Wanting and doing are two very different matters. Failure to be effective often comes from a lack of very ordinary tools or the ability to use them. In fact, few people seem to know how to *identify and use effectively* what they already have: their personal traits, physical attributes, hard-earned skills, talents, profound insights, and wonderfully interesting experiences and stories.

## Self, Our Most Important Tool

Since the self is the most important tool always at hand in ministering, we must have confidence in using it. First of all, we must know who we are and what we have. The virtue of humility will help us because it helps us sort out our positive and negative features. Since it counsels us to know and accept the truth about ourselves, it speaks of our strengths, weaknesses, talents, and limitations.

Seldom do we give ourselves credit for who we are and what we have. Elderly parishioners, for example, with a lifetime of accumulated experience, wisdom, and stories are truly the "elders" of our parishes. Each of us is someone special. We are sons, daughters, parents, grandparents, friends, persons with all kinds of human and professional skills. We have hobbies and creative interests. We are homespun interior decorators, gardeners, readers, television critics, poets, storytellers, hikers, and so on. Ministry slots in the parish would benefit from one or more of these human interest areas. Once we get a handle on these important tools of ministry, confidence urges us to use them for the reign of God.

Personality characteristics differ from person to person, but we all have them. They are part of our real self as we minister to others and are, in fact, part of our ministry tool kit. They develop early in life and become habits by using them through the years. We notice such positive traits in others but not as often in ourselves: the natural tendencies to be patient, kind, affectionate, loving, caring, smiling, affirming, understanding, creative, hard-working, insightful, and wise. Our ministry efforts benefit from these personality traits as much as from the best formation sessions and workshops.

Besides these positive traits, we have the gift of faith with experiences of salvation, sin, conversion, and perhaps even intense religious experiences. We have logged hundreds of hours of listening to Scripture readings and homilies. We have done our share of searching for God and have enjoyed moments when we found God. In fact, our preparation for ministry is not essentially different from what the apostles had.

What we already have can make us confident. It provides us with the fundamentals to meet the situation at hand. The challenge is to identify our personal tools and to use them. Then, as we gain more and more experience, the challenge is to use ever more fully what we already have while developing the new skills we would like to have.

## Coming to Grips with Our Dark Side

That is the good news about being confident. There is some bad news, too. We are people who also have a dark side. This perhaps more than anything else makes us feel inadequate to take part in parish ministries. We have personality traits we would like to hide under a bushel. There is sin in our life; there are weaknesses in our relationships; we are frequently less than thrilled with our God and with our church. Personality defects and weaknesses in our religious and moral development limit the effectiveness of our ministry. Unfortunately, we are usually more aware of our dark side than our bright side.

The challenge of sharing in the church's ministries can be the occasion for coming to grips with our dark side. In doing so, we increase our confidence. Some of the most effective parish ministers are people who have experienced years of personal and spiritual darkness and even separation from the church.

Other limitations that threaten our confidence are related to our lack of skills needed in ministry. We must be open to pursue further formation, education, and skill development. We also need to know when to rely on others to supply what we lack, as we supply what they may lack. This is an obvious example of the importance—and benefit—of team ministry. It is helpful to remember that we are called to be a *part* of the Body of Christ, not the whole body, regardless of what anyone expects of us.

Constraints within our ministry also might threaten our confidence. Some situations may not allow us maximum use of our gifts and skills. For example, we may be skilled public speakers, but institutional constraints (parish or diocesan regulations) prevent us from preaching homilies or limit other speaking opportunities.

Besides the constraints from church law or local custom, some arise within a particular situation of ministry. We may be prevented from using our gifts because of the personalities of team members, the limited range of our ministry job description, or the reluctance of the parish to accept certain forms of ministries. Some parishes are more hesitant than others to accept or experiment with new ideas and new ministries. We need to assess accurately the context of our ministry and proceed accordingly. Even parishes resisting change will mellow and accept new ideas and ministries if they are not pushed too far too fast.

Our confidence grows when we are encouraged and praised by members of the team and by the people we serve. On the other hand, it easily erodes when others are overly negative and critical. While positive strokes are essential to healthy ministry, the firm anchor of confidence will always be a composite of a healthy self-image, competence, and professionalism. Then, when criticism comes, as it surely will, when encouragement and praise are in short supply, we can put all in context and not be at the mercy of others' good will or ill will.

Although criticism or lack of appreciation might threaten our confidence, either can also contribute to our effectiveness, challenging us to evaluate our ministry style and improve weak areas. But we should not use criticism to provide direction for personal improvement. That should always come from our own sense of identity, our call to ministry, and our lavish personal gifts.

Finally, the presence of the Lord and the Spirit God sends, above all else, should make us confident: "Remember, I am with you always, to the end of the age" (Matthew 28:20). ". . . the Advocate, the Holy Spirit, whom the Father will send in my name, will teach you everything, and remind you of all that I have said to you" (John 14:26). God's guidance and support comes with any call to church ministry. This powerful presence of God, however, does not replace our flesh-and-blood selves through which God continues to touch people. Unless this self comes through in our ministry to others, everything else tends to be fake, superficial, and ineffective.

## Questions for Reflection and Discussion

1. About what do you feel most inadequate in your ministry? Most confident?

2. List as fully as possible your positive qualities and traits. Include ordinary and special gifts, skills, interests, and experiences, etc.

3. Who was the most effective parish minister you have known? What qualities did that person have that you admired the most? Which of these do you have—or would like to have?

4. What nice things have been said about you? (Ask someone who knows you to describe your positive qualities.) Which of these qualities are helpful in your ministry?

5. Write a sentence full of positive adjectives that describe yourself.

6. List some qualities that you would like to develop further.

7. Describe some negative personal qualities you would like to change.

8. On the basis of this reflection, write a personal goal related to your confidence to serve in ministry.

# — 13 —

# Imagination and Creativity
# in Ministry

## Imagination and Its Function in Religion

Imagination, a much underappreciated faculty, is just as important and potentially as effective as our other powers of intellect, will, movement, and senses. We use it to discover or expand reality, to gain new and deeper insights into what is already real. To do this, we use what is available to our senses, emotions, and environment. We refashion reality, recreating it until something new, fresh, and exciting emerges. In this sense, imagination functions like our dreams when our subconscious reaches out and gathers, so to speak, whatever is available in the subconscious pool, creating new images and story plots. The difference is that imagination functions on the conscious level and is pretty much under our control; it is at our service.

Our imagination is a bridge we walk across between the familiar details of our everyday life and what lies beyond them. We go from the concrete details of our daily life into the dimension of mystery, enjoying a deeper level of truth, the truly real world.

The following testimony from a lay minister shows how easily the natural process of imagination touches religion:

Recently I visited the little country church where I had been baptized as an infant and in whose shadows I had lived until I was a teen. As I walked around, looking at the stained glass windows, I noticed that none had titles. There were the typical memorial names of donors caught forever in the stained glass, already 135 years old, but nothing identified the scenes in the window. How did I know as a child, I wondered, that this one was the Annunciation? Another, the Visitation? Then I remembered. The pictures used to move! They used to be alive! The angel spoke to Mary. And Mary visited Elizabeth. I was looking at them now *without imagination.*

There can be no religion without imagination. More important still, there can be no faith without imagination. It is natural to picture what we believe; if we do not, religion becomes an abstraction, a head trip. Some theological literature, though very important, can be boring because the content does not evoke exciting images in our minds and affect our hearts.

Because an active imagination is so important to faith and religion, parish ministers should deliberately cultivate it in their own lives and make wise use of it in their ministry, including the judicious use of stories that resonate with the stories of the lives of others. One of the reasons fundamentalist groups and cults can be so effective is because they craft a particular religious world by feeding images to the imagination of compliant followers.

The use of imagination is scarcely a contemporary discovery. Imagination and the use of stories has always deeply influenced conventional Catholicism, and indeed all religions. Call to mind the images of hell fire, the Last Judgment, the evocative symbols associated with sacraments. The mysteries of the rosary become moving scenes in the life of Jesus and Mary. Stories about saints were as familiar as stories about relatives. What was lacking in the visuals in the Baltimore Catechism was more than made up for by the stories of preachers at parish missions. And those stained glass windows!

## Imagination and Ministry

We should remember as parish ministers that imagination does not function well in religious activities that emphasize only abstract truths about God. Concrete and sensual stuff is needed to stir us, to create new insights into what is real. Fortunately, most contemporary religious formation efforts, liturgy planning resources, and the media used by parish ministers cultivate the imagination. We have learned to invite people to know God through story: through Bible stories and through shared personal stories that touch our inmost depths. These provide a rich variety of images of the limitless divine mysteries. We invite people to know God experientially by finding divine presence within their real environment: in colors, in the transitions of natural and liturgical seasons, in rainbows, and seashores, and hugs, and flowers, and people. We invite people to find God in the labyrinths of their own personal stories.

The God we know today is not the result of an extraordinary vision that each of us has had. Rather, how we know God—our truly real God—is the result of our imagining. In a certain sense we create our own God.

If there were only one image of God, religious reality would be extremely limited and uninviting. Often when people rebel strongly against church experiences it is because they have been provided with a limited and unappealing image of God.

God is exciting. It just takes a little imagination.

## Creativity

Closely related to imagination is our ability to be creative. Creativity makes the difference between an exciting ministry and a merely functional one. It can be described as the thrill of going down new roads and thoroughly enjoying the trip. It is giving in to the magnetic pull of the yet unknown, making real the yet uncreated possibilities of life and ministry. Creativity is finding mystery in ever new places.

Many people, parish ministers included, live their lives in straight lines: the shortest distance, as it were, between birth and death. Such lives involve less risk, but also fewer delightful detours and side roads where exciting experiences and people are waiting to be encountered. These straight, narrow lives do avoid much heartache, tension, conflict, and perhaps even sin. At the same time, straight-line living avoids challenges that deepen love, nurture faith, provide excitement, and enrich one's personality and therefore ministry. In the final analysis, straight-line living avoids what makes life worth living: risk and creativity.

All human life, even straight-line living, has to wander down some side roads. The very nature of relationships, family life, religious convictions, and professional careers require occasional deviations from the straight and narrow, from the usual and ordinary. When this happens there is a choice: one can make the "side road" either a joy or a function. The choice will result in a life that is either creative and exciting or merely functional.

What is true of life in general is true also of each responsibility we take upon ourselves, including ministry. Without doubt, this responsibility of ministry will take us down roads we have not traveled before, away from our usual way of parenting, working, and believing. This new road can be either a joy or merely a new function. If it becomes just another function, our tendency will be to do it with the least amount of energy—another "thing" we were talked into, another activity to get through and fit into our already busy lives. Our ministry will tend to be hurried, lifeless, and tedious. If, on the other hand, we consider this side road called ministry a joy, a different atmosphere permeates our efforts: the thrill of challenge, a new purpose, risk, excitement, change, personal growth, and unlimited new experiences.

Creative ministry should be enjoyable—fun. Only when ministry is reduced to tasks and functions does it become a chore. Functional ministry exhausts; creative ministry restores our spirit and generates enthusiasm. To be enthusiastic means to be filled with spirit: human spirit and God's Spirit. Where there is spirit, there is life and joy. Where spirit is lacking, there is only a job to be done, tasks to be performed. And the tasks are endless, so it seems, leading only to exhaustion because the spirit is not renewed.

Many of us stick to functional activity, avoiding creative opportunities, precisely because the functional is familiar and comfortable. We do not have to deal with the unknown. Creative ministry, therefore, can frighten us, especially when a previously functional person steps into the unknown—for the first time.

> The creative process is also the most terrifying part because you don't know exactly what's going to happen or where it is going to lead. You don't know what new dangers and challenges you'll find. It takes an enormous amount of internal security to begin with the spirit of adventure, the spirit of discovery, the spirit of creativity. Without doubt, you have to leave the comfort zone of base camp and confront an entirely new and unknown wilderness. You become a trailblazer, a pathfinder. You open new possibilities, new territories, new continents, so that others can follow (Covey, *The Seven Habits of Highly Effective People*, p. 263).

Every person possesses the quality of creativity. We are born with it, and during childhood we were intently and unselfconsciously creative. But as we grew up, creativity was not challenged and exercised enough and it tended to atrophy. So, it is not a matter of becoming creative, but rather of *reactivating* what is already within us. Creativity is not limited to great composers, artists, and writers, or to being handy at crafts. These are only *some* expressions of creativity.

Many of us stopped being creative when the functional approach was emphasized and even drilled by parents, teachers, and supervisors. Our culture, too, tends to promote functionalism and downplay creativity. So does the work environment and the expectations of management in employment.

Culture and institutions demand conformity because it is easier to control people who conform. Truly creative people are notorious for being difficult to control; they tend to be non-conformists. In some quarters they are even considered dangerous because of their unnerving tendency to avoid conformity to expected behavior and to challenge and undermine the status quo. Fortunately, when creativity is squelched, it only goes underground; it is not lost forever. We can resurrect it by doing things we enjoy, by being open to new possibilities, new approaches, new opportunities.

Jesus was creative, as were the great leaders the world has known. In society and its institutions they exercised their creativity in such a way that they were able to inspire and lead. And they could do this because they could see situations from new perspectives and with new possibilities; they saw opportunities where others saw only closed doors.

Creativity gives us the ability to make the most of the present, to draw out its possibilities, and to dream of even better things for the future. "You see things that are and say, 'Why?' But I dream of things that never were and say, 'Why not?'" (George Bernard Shaw)

We all know creative people, some participating in continuing education programs, some expanding their creativity by reading, some doing marvelous things with their hands, some with the written word. We might suspect that these creative people are also dreaming a lot. Sometimes we rashly judge them for wasting time and neglecting their responsibilities (or functions). We hardly ever, however, hear a creative person complain about the extra time, effort, and discipline that creative work takes. In fact, they speak enthusiastically about it: the thrill of challenge, their new experiences and experiments, their new creations. It is the overly functional person who is more likely to complain of new demands because they interfere with straight-line living and ministering.

What kind of creativity is involved in the great variety of lay ministries? Where is the thrill of going down new roads and thoroughly enjoying the trip? Creativity is very personal and, therefore, differs for each. It cannot be assigned by the pastor or other administrator, nor copied from someone else. Only functions can be assigned or copied. Some examples might get us highly functional people to risk a little. First of all, down what "side road" do we seem to be naturally drawn? Down what "side roads" does our ministry commitment seem to be drawing us? Any side trip, freely taken with a touch of excitement, will have an impact on our ministry. It does not have to have obvious religious overtones.

Becoming more creative might call for deliberate discipline, reading, research, and continuing education. The diocese or parish, local colleges, and school districts have resource libraries and manifold educational opportunities.

Creativity does not have as its goal the completion of new projects. It is a human quality that affects all we do. It has the power to expand our lives and our ministry in such a way that we are no longer merely adequate. By daring to go down side roads, we can enjoy what the Lord invites us to: fullness of life, for ourselves and those we minister to. A creative minister is a creative person.

## Discernment

We described creativity as "the thrill of going down new roads and thoroughly enjoying the trip." We will find mystery down those new roads. Usually it is easier to look back and find mystery and meaning in the trips we have already taken. Looking ahead is not always easy. Each time we begin an important segment of life's many journeys and side roads, we have a beginning point and a desired destination. That much is usually evident. Seldom, though, do we have a precise roadmap that assures us that we will make the trip without getting lost several times. Not that we have a lack of would-be guides along the way. Indeed, the opposite is true. Many voices clamor for our attention: "Come this way . . . Come here . . . go there . . . this way . . . no, that way . . . this way is blocked." It is easy to become confused, especially if we lack a sense of direction.

Like a wise hiker with a compass, we, too, have several resources to give us a continual reading of our position and direction. An informed sense of Scripture is one resource. Another is our community of faith, especially the persons of wisdom in the community.

We also have another resource: a wisdom deep within that lets us know whether our current direction is truly compatible with who we are and what our life is all about. Or, is our current direction incompatible with our truest self? This inner wisdom becomes evident, first of all, in our "gut," in our physical and nervous systems. If we fail to sit at the feet of this wisdom and heed it, it has unique ways of getting our attention with all kinds of physical illness and mental stress.

This process of keeping in touch with our resources as we chart our direction is *discernment*. It is the process of figuring out—intuiting?—the best way(s) to follow the voice of the One who calls us and walks with us. We discern God's will for us, the direction God wants us to take, by listening attentively to our desires and discontent, to our delights and frustrations, to our sense of peace and inner harmony, to our inner turmoil and lack of peace. What we feel intensely in our inmost being often takes a long time to get through to our head. In fact, sometimes we are so out of touch with our own feelings that they never get through to our decision-making center.

When should we worry that our choices are not in conformity with God's will? When they lead us away from such basic gospel patterns as love, generosity, and service. Or when we reject basic doctrinal and moral traditions that have stood the test of time. Or when our decisions lead us down paths that are isolated and eccentric. Or when we deliberately avoid the counsel and information available from mentors and other qualified leaders in our faith community.

As much as we would like a specific map to follow, a good, dependable human guide to rely on, we might first of all rely on the One who is both our guide and destination. God often leads us in surprising directions, which do not always make sense. That is the wonder—and fun—of the trip!

As we learn to grow in faith and trust the One who leads us by walking with us down all kinds of wonderful side roads, we begin to tap into God's dream for us (see Chapter 24, Tapping into God's Dream), a dream that is beyond our imagination and yet completely in harmony with who we are and who we are called to be. That is the mystery of our life.

## Questions for Reflection and Discussion
1. How much does your imagination add to your favorite biblical stories?

2. Choose three images of God with which you are most comfortable. How is imagination part of your choosing? Would your peers choose the same images?

3. Reflect on a creative venture in your ministry that you were particularly pleased with. Was it a joy rather than function? In what ways were you more fully alive during this venture?

4. Review your recent ministry efforts. Have any been significantly creative? In what way?

5. Chart your usual process of discerning what new roads to travel, new paths to explore in your life and ministry.

6. What aspect of your current ministry do you feel calls for discernment on your part?

# — 14 —

# Being Comfortable
# with Our Place

### Collaborative Ministry in the Body of Christ

Ministry today is more often than not a shared, or collaborative, effort. The very word "collaborative" says it all: from the Latin for "working together." This style of ministry benefits from our contemporary culture, primarily the world of business. It is obvious that much more can be accomplished effectively when a number of people are involved, and each does his or her share.

Collaborative ministry may take several forms. A pastoral *staff* retains elements of rank, with someone in charge, such as a supervisor or administrator. This administrator has persons with specific job descriptions reporting to her or him. In turn, administrators are usually responsible to someone with still higher authority. On a pastoral *team*, ministers function more interdependently, planning together, sharing insights and responsibilities, and meeting on a regular basis to keep ministry efforts coordinated. While no one need be officially in charge, there is usually a team leader responsible for preparing agendas and presiding at meetings.

From the beginning, Christians had to struggle with the challenges that accompany a community effort. They stumbled often in the face of competing traditions and even had to contend with claims to special rank. Paul had to help them come to grips with this. We can imagine him becoming enthusiastic about the image he was using to describe the mystery of unity and diversity within the ever-expanding community of followers of Jesus. A strong intensity is evident in Paul as the image evolves. It seems to go places that not even Paul had originally anticipated. He paces rapidly, dictating to his secretary:

> For as the body is one and has many members, and all the members of the body, though many, are one body, so it is with Christ. For in the one Spirit we were all baptized into one body—Jews or Greeks, slaves or free—and we are all made to drink of one Spirit.
>
> Indeed, the body does not consist of one member but of many. If the foot would say, "Because I am not a hand, I do not belong to the body," that would not make it any less a part of the body. And if the ear would say, "Because I am not an eye, I do not belong to the body," that would not make it any less a part of the body. If the whole body were an eye, where would the hearing be? If the whole body were hearing, where would the sense of smell be? But as it is, God arranged the members in the body, each one of them, as he chose. If all were a single member, where would the body be? As it is, there are many members, yet one body. The eye cannot say to the hand, "I have no need of you," nor again the head to the feet, "I have no need of you." On the contrary, the members of the body that seem to be weaker are indispensable, and those members of the body that we think less honorable we clothe with greater honor, and our less respectable members are treated with greater respect, whereas our more respectable members do not need this. But God has so arranged the body, giving the greater honor to the inferior member, that there may be no dissension within the body, but the members may have the same care for one another. If one member suffers, all suffer together with it; if one member is honored, all rejoice together with it (1 Corinthians 12:12–26).

Paul's image is as fresh and insightful 2000 years later as the day he first dictated it. He will excuse us if we expand upon his analogy to discuss the value of a variety of shared ministries in the same parish community.

Whenever a group of parishioners (for example, a pastoral team, a parish council, a worship commission, or an ad hoc committee) assemble to plan an activity or ministry, someone invariably says: "Put me down for _____, because I can't do _____." Most of the time this is an honest self-evaluation based on years of experience, on an awareness of what we can do well. Besides this insight into our ability, there is the fact that we simply enjoy doing some things and dislike doing others. Yet we seem embarrassed to admit that we cannot do everything or do not enjoy doing everything.

The fact is that some of us are "feet" in the body of Christ; ask us to run an errand and we are on our way. Some of us are "hands"; we like to do the practical stuff of cooking, making banners, setting up tables, and perhaps doing some painting, electrical wiring, or carpentry.

Then there are the "eyes" and "ears" of the local faith community. These are the people who have a knack of noticing what needs to be done or how the body might function better. They see and hear a good deal and share their insights with decision makers. They may not be able to do the practical things and make the practical changes that they have observed need doing. That is not their gift, nor does it need to be their function in the body that is the church.

We might carry Paul's analogy a little further and include other parts and functions of the body. Some of us are thinkers. We relate better to the brain of the body than to other parts of it. We think well; we like to discuss and interpret what the "eyes" see and "ears" hear. But don't ask us to be responsible for a parish meal. We might come up with various reasons for a special parish agape—but cooks we are not. The parish community will be better off if some special "hands" do that.

It would not be good for the local faith community if all its members had the same gifts and inclinations. ". . . where would the body be?" We need the eyes and ears, those who keep us aware of where we need to go, and the thinkers or planners who show us the creative ways to get there. We need the hands and feet of those who carry out practical aspects of ministries or do many of the practical chores. We also need those who are identified by Paul as those who, at first glance, might seem to be less important parts: those who clean up after the thinkers and doers are finished!

## Shared Ministry: The Better Way to Go

We would be gravely mistaken if we consider shared ministry, or team ministry, a practical necessity only because of an increasing shortage of clergy. Some people feel that while we had enough priests we did not "need" lay ministers. And when we have enough again down the road, we will not "need" them again. Shared ministry is a sound biblical and theological issue. Laity are in ministry because of who we *are*, not because of a shortage of clergy or religious.

Rademacher describes at length seven biblical/theological foundations for shared ministry. In summary: 1) A community that shares the bread and cup, *koinonia*, should share ministry, 2) Paul's image of the body of Christ (Ephesians 4:11–12; 1 Corinthians 12:12–26; Romans 12:4–8), 3) common discipleship of all the baptized, 4) common possession of the Spirit, 5) common possession of the one priesthood of Christ (1 Peter 2:9), 6) common mission flowing from shared baptism and confirmation, 7) pastoral collegiality. (See Rademacher, pp. 169-175.)

At first, it would seem that shared, or team, ministry would always make things easier for us. The contrary is often true. Sometimes it is easier to be a "lone ranger." Perhaps that is why there have been so many of them in ministry: no one to answer to, no one to adjust procedures for, no one to get under foot and undo what you have done.

While not always easier, shared ministry is always better, and most often more effective. No one has all the answers, gifts, creative ideas, and the most effective methodology. Shared ministry introduces us to a pool of resources: charisms, talents, personalities, methodologies.

If a ministry team functions well and maturely, each person has the opportunity to evolve into a more effective—and holier—minister. We find that we are more whole when in union with others. We begin to learn from our mistakes instead of perpetuating them. We find that each person on the team contributes something unique to the shared efforts; each has a richness of personality and gifts that differs from the others'.

It is very helpful if a team of ministers takes the time to discover the variety and richness of approaches that come naturally to each one. The Myers-Briggs Personality Profile is an excellent tool for both personal and team insights. A ministry team will function more harmoniously and productively if they know and understand one another's personality characteristics. A simple version of the Myers-Briggs Personality Profile is the Keirsey-Bates Sorter. (See *Please Understand Me*, 1984, or Keating, *Who We Are Is How We Pray*, 1987.) Another excellent personality profile is the Enneagram. (See Éilís and Fitzgerald, *An Enneagram Guide*, 1993.)

Besides our own personality, each of us brings to the team an agenda, a composite self, with our own operating philosophy, core beliefs, intellectual and moral foundations, view of the local and universal church, and our own functioning religious identity. (See Chapter 11, Clarifying Our Religious Identity.) In shared ministry we have an ongoing opportunity to balance all of this with what others bring to the team. Regular meetings allow us to try out possible goals and plans. If we avoid this sharing and get out too far away from others, we may very well wind up going our separate ways, thus becoming ineffective. As mature ministers who make decisions and take initiatives and prudent risks, we will be effective only if we work with others during all phases of our work. We will adjust our efforts and change our directions according to the positive suggestions of others, which has the added benefit of having team support behind our efforts.

## Giving Our Best

Because shared ministry promotes the reign of God, we bring to our ministerial activities the best we can. Haass (*The Power to Persuade*, 1994), writing from years of experience in high levels of government in Washington, D.C., makes a good case for the fact that effective service in government is not all that different from service in other human institutions, including not-for-profit organizations. Therefore, techniques to achieve excellence in secular service will benefit our ministry to make visible the saving power and love of God. He describes thirteen of these techniques (pp. 44-69). A paraphrase of them will serve us well.

1. Pledge yourself to excellence. Ordinarily it is better to do nothing at all than to do something poorly. This means paying attention to the little things. We never allow pride or arrogance to prevent us from doing what we know is right.

2. Never assume anything. We always have to be prepared for the unexpected and unprecedented because that is what usually happens!

3. Do not be afraid to act. It is very important that we do our homework and be well prepared, but at some point we have to just do it.

4. Use only those plans and policies that can be implemented. On paper they can be intellectually beautiful and persuasive, but we have to be able to get them done. An idea is not good if it won't work.

5. Never cut corners. And keep your word and be straight with people.

6. Do your homework and master the material. We will tend to do well if we know the issue at hand. This means that we subject our decisions to the most rigorous analysis and make sure they stand up to the test of implementation.

7. Control your schedule. We will be more effective if we control our time and energy. There is a limit on how many things we can do and an even greater limit on how many we can do well.

8. Set aside time to think. We should leave some time every day to reflect on what we are doing and how we are doing it, and what we might not be paying attention to and should.

9. Be prepared to work hard. There is no substitute for perseverance, even against odds.

10. Be decent to people. If we have a deserved reputation for being polite, our effectiveness will increase. The opposite kind of reputation will defeat our best efforts and intentions.

11. Be careful. Everything we worked hard to achieve can be jeopardized by one serious lapse of judgment or one cut corner.

12. Keep your perspective. We should never take ourselves more seriously than necessary. A little bit of humility will go a long way. We should be good to ourselves. We should set aside time for our personal life, for friends, for family, and for health. (See Chapter 19, Ministering with Wholistic Patterns.)

13. Keep lists. There is no better way to keep track of all that we must do. None of us has a perfect memory.

## Questions for Reflection and Discussion

1. Reflect upon Paul's analogy of the body (1 Corinthians 12:12–26). Which part do you most relate to? Why? When did you function best as this "member" of the body of Christ?

2. If you know your Myers-Briggs readout or your Enneagram, how does it match your self-identification with this member of the body? (See question 1.)

3. Is your ministry team a *functioning* body? Without negative judgment, reflect upon your parish leadership (team, council, commissions, committees). What parts of the body would you relate various leaders to?

4. Invite the persons you minister with to make a cut-out of a member of the body they identify with. Then put the "body" togeth-

er. Is the "body" out of balance? Is this an accurate diagram of the group?

5. How well do you function with other members of the body—team or staff?

6. If you have had experience in the secular world, what of value have you carried over into your church ministry?

# — 15 —

# Ministering Effectively
# with Others

We noted in the previous chapter that effective ministry is shared ministry—planned, coordinated, and carried out with others. Team ministry is not just a buzz word. Because a characteristic of mature humans is to function together, ministry is more effective when shared. Shared ministry also reflects the community nature of the church. What is more effective and theologically sound, however, is not necessarily easier. In fact, team ministry brings a host of new challenges.

## Being Effective Administrators
Many ministers have chosen or accepted an assignment to administer programs of a church community with supervisory or management responsibilities. Scripture writers were experienced with a church in its earliest stages of evolution; there is not much in Scripture, then, to serve as practical guidelines in highly developed church structures in dioceses and parishes and the multiple ministries functioning in them. Fidelity to Jesus' golden rule of discipleship will go far to keep administrators effective, happy, and in good relationship with personnel reporting to them: "Do to others as you would have them do to you" (Luke 6:31).

Obviously, this needs to be fleshed out. Few ministers are experts in group dynamics and administration. While we may have natural and Spirit-given gifts, we still have to work hard to develop the skills and techniques necessary for our profession. Once again we can turn to the techniques and skills that have proven effective in the world of business and government. Some of these are found in *The Power to Persuade* (pp. 102-150). The following is a summary of them; the context is that of a functioning staff, rather than a team.

As effective administrators, we need to be much more than desk persons or bosses. We should be leaders who can motivate people to perform their responsibilities as well as possible to achieve goals and objectives.

We should look upon staff as partners in ministry. Listening carefully to them is key to effective administration. We do not have to agree with everything we hear, but we must provide an atmosphere in which the insights and convictions of others are welcome. We cannot hear if we are always talking. Speaking too soon, or too much, will stifle the voices of others. Eventually, however, only one person can make a decision and that is the person in authority.

When we choose to move on to new responsibilities or to a new parish, we should be careful of this critical transition time. We can make a first impression only once. Colleagues who will report to us and superiors who will evaluate us will be scrutinizing what we do and what we say. The style of our arrival is therefore important. There is nothing too insignificant to ignore during transition. We need to communicate clearly what we will emphasize: continuity or change. Structural change, however, should always be a means to an important end and not an end in itself.

Wise administrators should not have to resort to ordering staff in every detail. We should create the kind of environment in which the women and men we supervise feel like our partners and feel free to share their ideas, no matter how much they may differ from our own. This kind of open environment will promote outstanding performance because the ministry we are supervising will be *owned* by many. We should roam freely and comfortably in the ministry areas rather than hiding out in an inner office.

Respond quickly to the needs and questions of staff. Know their strengths and weaknesses—and needs. Each person needs something different to perform effectively. Learn what each needs; ordinarily these are very human and understandable, such as praise, public acknowledgment, or credit for work well done. These simple but gracious actions are doubly important because material rewards of ministry are limited. Criticism should always be done privately.

Be consistent. Avoid decisions and actions that catch staff off guard. Changing course too often will confuse and demoralize them.

Manage by example. What we do will have as much if not more impact than what we say or the memos we issue. Always be willing to join in practical ministry efforts.

Hold regular staff meetings, preferably short ones. They provide a necessary sounding board for feelings, an opportunity to clarify direction of efforts, and an opportunity for staff interaction. They will also ensure that the staff has necessary, current information. More formal meetings should be scheduled when we need to develop ideas or to deal with pressing serious issues.

Wise administrators delegate what can be or should be taken care of by staff. This prevents exhaustion and allows us to put our efforts into fewer but more important matters and priorities of office. Too much delegation, however, will weaken administration if it causes us to lose touch with our own responsible ministry. When we do delegate, it is important that we set up mechanisms to monitor what is being done.

Be loyal to your staff. Shield them from unjust criticism. Provide opportunities for them to develop their skills and ministry careers.

Meet privately with individual staff members periodically. Use these opportunities to review performance.

Sometimes it is necessary to terminate someone's ministry because of poor performance. Deal with this situation of performance early. It is unfair to terminate someone without warnings, preferably written, which provide opportunity to change the situation. Termination of ministry can cause all kinds of ugliness; to prevent this, document all communications made to the person.

## Ministering Effectively with Colleagues

Whether we share ministry on a team or staff, we are functioning in relationship with someone else. Even in the most intimate of relationships, marriage for example, joint effort is frequently difficult and some tension and conflict inevitable. All the more so when we try to mesh efforts, convictions, and methodologies with colleagues.

We should be faithful to a few rules for effective joint ministry. We should make every effort to *know* our colleagues: something of their history, likes and dislikes, current family situation, hobbies, interests outside of ministry, ministry experience, theological attitudes, prayer styles, and particular hurts, past and present, that are an important part of their story and can affect their emotional moods and ministry effectiveness. This information should come informally by way of sincere listening, an attitude of openness, allowing others to know us. There should be an atmosphere of trust, support, and confidentiality. Meetings and occasional prayer sessions should provide an opportunity to share personal stories.

We should have accurate information about the ministry job description of each of our colleagues and they should know what ours is. Confusions about expectations, responsibilities, and limits should be clarified immediately at team or staff meetings.

We should not get hung up on seniority, rank, or credentials. Nor should we ally ourselves only with colleagues who tend to agree with our theological convictions and methods of ministry. If we listen sincerely to other viewpoints and compromise on non-essentials, a more comprehensive and collaborative ministry can evolve. It may not be formed totally to our expectations, but there may be more of a consensus, and the quality of decision making may improve. On the other hand, we should be wise enough to know when colleagues "have an attitude" about something and nothing constructive to contribute. When there is a total impasse, basic methods of conflict resolution should be used. In very serious situations, an outside facilitator should be brought in.

## Questions for Reflection and Discussion

1. Reflect upon your most pleasant and/or effective ministry under someone's authority and supervision. What effective characteristics did this administrator have?

2. Then reflect upon your most unpleasant and/or ineffective ministry. To what extent was an administrator responsible for this? To what extent was your own ministry style responsible?

3. What are the most positive features of your own administration? Most negative?

4. What are the positive features of your relationship with colleagues? Negative features? Conflicts?

5. How do you tend to resolve conflict situations?

# — 16 —

# When
# Theologies Clash

### Sharing a Hierarchy of Truths

We saw in Chapter 11 that practical matters of religious faith are not identical for all Catholics. Parishioners and those designated as their ministers often have strong feelings about which religious truths (in many cases only half-truths) and religious traditions should be emphasized and promoted by way of parish ministries. Unfortunately, these priorities are seldom worked out deliberately. Nor are they always based on profound religious experiences. More often they are *presumed* priorities because of an inherited religious identity and personal religious biases. Sometimes religious priorities are influenced by preachers, popular magazines, and other, unofficial channels of faith formation. The consequence might be a preoccupation with a particular religious reality without taking its relative importance into consideration. Or, no effort is made to distinguish between essentials and non-essentials within the very broad, rich Catholic tradition.

What is important to individual parishioners does not always match what is important to the parish team and other parish leaders. This "mismatch" sometimes leads to conflict as individuals, even on the same ministry team, emphasize, or insist, that others adopt and practice what is important to *them*. Some will even spy on and criticize what seems to them to be out of kilter in a parish's ministry activities.

Disagreement about what is essential and important in religious belief and behavior was an affliction even in first-generation Christianity. In most early centers of Christianity there were serious clashes about the relative—or essential—importance of maintaining and observing Jewish traditions:

But because of false believers secretly brought in, who slipped in to spy on the freedom we have in Christ Jesus, so that they might enslave us—we did not submit to them even for a moment, so that the truth of the gospel might always remain with you (Galatians 2:4ff).

Failure to respect a hierarchy within religious truths on the part of designated ministers can be very damaging to the whole parish community. Fortunately, most parish leaders and parishioners do choose religious truths high in the church's deposit of faith upon which to build a spirituality that influences their daily life and meets the challenges of baptism and gospel. Some, however, do not have a clear grasp of religious priorities at all.

There *is* a hierarchy of religious truths and practices in both a popular and official sense; some Catholic teachings and traditions are of greater importance than others, although all are related to faith. This has always been the case in the history of the church.

Catholic bishops have repeatedly expressed concern about priorities among religious truths as they relate to religious formation. Church authority recognizes that the ministry of catechetics is critical in forming a Catholic religious identity. In union with Vatican offices, they have been concerned with possible fragmentation within the church at large. Their attempts to maintain unity have resulted in numerous documents and guidelines concerning the theory and practice of catechesis. The most recent effort on the part of the Vatican is the *Catechism of the Catholic Church* promulgated by Pope John Paul II in 1992 and published in English in 1994.

Other important documents have been published over the past generation. They are the *General Catechetical Directory*, prepared by the Sacred Congregation for the Clergy and approved by Pope Paul VI in 1971; *To Teach as Jesus Did: A Pastoral Message on Catholic Education*, prepared by the National Conference of Catholic Bishops, 1972; *Basic Teachings for Catholic Religious Education*, prepared by the National Conference of Catholic Bishops in consultation with the Holy See, 1973; and *Sharing the Light of Faith: National Catechetical Directory for Catholics of the United States* (NCD), prepared by the National Conference of Catholic Bishops and approved by the Sacred Congregation for the Clergy in 1979.

This last document, the NCD, repeats a traditional four-fold grouping of essential religious truths: 1) the mystery of God the Father, the Son, and the Holy Spirit, Creator of all things; 2) the mystery of Christ, the incarnate Word, who was born of the Virgin Mary, and who suffered, died, and rose for our salvation; 3) the mystery of the Holy Spirit, who is present in the church, sanctifying it and guiding it until the glorious coming of Christ, our Savior and Judge; 4) the mystery of the church, which is Christ's Mystical Body, in which the Virgin Mary holds the preeminent place. (See *General Catechetical Directory*, 43.)

Chapter Five of the NCD, "Principal Elements of the Christian Message for Catechesis," develops these basic religious truths by way of ten categories, providing us with a convenient hierarchy of truth: one God, creation, Jesus Christ, the Holy Spirit, the church, the sacraments, the life of grace, the moral life, Mary and the saints, and death, judgment, and eternity. (See *Sharing the Light of Faith*, 24.)

Another document has touched the very center and soul of religious formation, the *Rite of Christian Initiation of Adults*—RCIA (1972). This document has ushered in a renewed emphasis, as people come to faith, on the role of Scripture, personal story, and the support of the believing community. This process will continue to have great impact on the religious priorities of parishioners and how people of all ages come to and grow in faith.

We need not run constantly to church documents to find religious priorities. Church practice offers a good guide for clarifying our religious priorities. The unfolding of the *church year* is such a guide. One exciting liturgical season evolves out of another as the presence of mystery ebbs and flows through our life. The church's official three-year cycle of Scripture readings holds all together as our Catholic traditions keep repeating who we are. The center of all is the Easter season, which proclaims that the heart of our religious faith and spirituality is life, new life, and a messiah who is risen and Lord. Our own initiation into faith, regardless of when it happened, is related to this Easter moment and should rank high in our religious priorities.

## Dealing with Conflicting Religious Priorities

Even though some truths of faith enjoy a higher priority than others, not all Catholics, obviously, share exactly the same priorities in their religious faith and spirituality. The same is true of a parish ministry team. It is important, however, that a person's basic religious identity be founded on major priority religious truths. When this is the case, a pluralism expressive of lesser elements of Catholic tradition will be tolerated more easily. Belief in and sharing in the

Eucharist is a higher priority truth than praying the rosary, even though the latter is also a good religious practice.

It is not hard to figure out that there are essentials and non-essentials within the very extensive body of Catholic teaching and traditions. If we are to choose a religious truth upon which to build a spirituality that influences our daily life and leads us to meet the challenges of baptism and gospel, then this truth should be of high priority in the church's catechesis. For example, Jesus' mandate that we respond to the needs of the poor commands a higher priority than private revelations and visions, whatever their content. The location of the baptismal font or pool is more important than the location of the votive stand.

We must also keep in mind that in regard to religious truths many Catholics separate on the basis of a pre- and post-Vatican II mindset. This influences one's concept of who God is and how God relates to us. Is God a harsh judge? A traffic cop deity? Or a loving parent? Is Mary a passive, submissive, docile woman? Or is she a strong, down-to-earth woman, deeply in touch with God and open to the mysteries unfolding in her own life? It is important that we can identify another person's mindset and its origin. It is also important that we are able to accept others as they are instead of quickly writing them off because we do not agree with their convictions or their images of God.

There are no magic solutions to conflicting religious priorities, whether these happen on the pastoral team or between parish ministers and parishioners. The following guidelines might help:

1. *Admit and affirm what is true.* For example, mysteries surrounding Mary, along with a wide variety of devotions to her, have been and still are a legitimate feature in contemporary Roman Catholicism. They are not, however, the highest priority and newer, more contemporary approaches to Marian devotions continue to evolve.

2. *Listen to their story.* Patiently get a clarification. What is the foundation of a particular conviction? What is the history of a particular religious identity? Is there any biblical or common church teaching related to the convictions that you can identify with and affirm? Or does the preoccupation concern a religious conviction that has no substantiation in reality or that has already been discounted by church authorities?

3. *Introduce the matter of a hierarchy of truths.* How much of their religious "energy" is spent on their particular preoccupation or con-

viction, and how much on practical ramifications of mysteries with a higher priority in the church's catechesis? For example, a group wants to plan a May Crowning on Pentecost weekend. Are they able to see a discrepancy? How do they justify their plans?

## Principles of Conflict Resolution

As noted above, there is widespread pluralism of religious convictions among Catholics. There is also pluralism about forms of ministry in the local parish. This pluralism causes conflict not only among parishioners, between parishioners and parish leaders and ministers, but also among these leaders and ministers serving on the same team or staff. Some basic principles of conflict resolution should be operational.

1. *Tolerance* should be a fundamental principle among Christians and their ministers. Otherwise, stress and conflict will cause further fragmentation. Only parish leaders and parishioners of open mind will foster the building up of the Body of Christ in the local parish. Tolerance encourages us to consider divergent views seriously without condemning or suppressing them. At the same time, we should remain true to our own convictions and act out of them while at the same time considering opposing views. The church is not finished yet, nor has the final word been spoken.

Tolerance is the bridge that brings together persons who are separated by conflict. Sometimes the heat of conflict cools when opposing viewpoints are permitted an airing or hearing. Not everyone will get their way, but everyone can have their say.

2. Another principle is *patience*. As Karl Rahner observed in discussing the matter of pluralism in the church, sometimes "all the Christian can do is come to terms with the situation, bear it patiently, and maintain in the church a unity which is effective in practice in spite of the difficulties involved" (*The Shape of the Church to Come*, p. 36).

3. Besides patience, Rahner suggests the need to *compromise*. He discusses the principle of dealing with conflict among factions in the Catholic church, which he calls "non-simultaneous groups," but without a "sham peace" and sometimes allowing for a "fair fight."

> . . . compromises simply cannot be avoided; they merely reflect the facts and try to do justice as far as possible to all these non-simultaneous groups. Since all the groups in principle certainly have a right to exist, the fact must be accepted in teaching

and in practice that in the one church with her one Spirit there can and must be a variety of charisms whose ultimate harmony perhaps simply cannot be fully experienced by us in the still continuing course of history; and [the Spirit] is not identical either with any sort of individual group or with the church's office-holders. The legitimacy of such compromises to maintain the church's unity in the diversity of historically non-simultaneous groups cannot, of course, mean a sham peace and does not remove the necessity of a fair fight among the groups. (Rahner, p. 36).

4. Rahner also emphasizes a need for _self-criticism._ Conflicting individuals or groups often exhibit a stubbornness as they try to legitimize their convictions and lobby for them. However, the harshness and even bitterness that accompanies the struggle can be kept within tolerable limits "if each group is self-critical and tries to understand the other group, if people are not too quick to deny the good will or genuine Christianity of both sides" (Rahner, p. 37).

This self-criticism does not mean that one's convictions are invalid. Methods used to express those convictions, however, are always open to question and critique. So, too, is one's personal attitude toward the "opposition party." For example, a particular group in the parish, or a faction of a parish team, out of love for tradition or opposition to diocesan liturgical guidelines, may oppose the pastor's or parish council's intentions to remodel their parish church along certain lines. This personal conviction—for them—is legitimate. From this point on, as each side separately and together works toward conflict resolution, self-criticism is of the highest importance. "Is it a legitimate Christian thing for us to gain control of the parish council for the express purpose of preventing the remodeling? To initiate a law suit against the bishop? To call in the secular press?" On the other hand, "Is it a legitimate Christian thing for us to hold secret meetings of the building committee to complete plans before the opposition can muster support?"

## Theological Reflection and Conflict Resolution

5. Conflicts regarding religious issues can also be resolved through _theological reflection._ This process goes beyond the few principles of conflict resolution just discussed, but presumes them. It is a _corporate_ process that is particularly helpful—and important—when the conflict concerns a very serious matter. "Corporate" emphasizes

that this is a *group* process, instead of the solitary—even though learned and specially experienced—voice. The question always is: "What is the group saying?" (For a comprehensive introduction to theological reflection, see Whitehead, *Method in Ministry*, Part One).

This process of theological reflection, which makes use of three sources of religiously relevant information—tradition, experience, and culture—is quite comprehensive and, therefore, an excellent tool in coming to grips with serious tensions and conflicts. It avoids the less than desirable "quick fix" approach. Its goal is not solely to promote a clarification of thinking within a group, though it does this, but to come to a pastoral decision or a ministerial response regarding a particular situation.

In this corporate process, the participants first of all identify all the information they can think of from tradition (Scripture, church history, church teaching) concerning a particular pastoral concern or stress issue. This is "tossed into the hopper" without deep reflection at this point. To this is added all the information available to the participants from their experience and from their culture and society that speaks to the issue under discussion. For example, in reflecting upon the role of the laity in a particular ministry, it would be naive to consider only past church discipline and traditions. The experience of the laity themselves and their giftedness played out in their cultural setting need to be considered as part of what the mystery of church is called to be today.

Once the relevant information has been gathered, the process continues:

A. Participants are given an opportunity to reflect privately on the issue(s) in light of the accumulated information.

B. The participants come together and share the fruits of this private reflection. The whole group listens—but does not discuss or debate at this time. Where does the group hear agreement?

C. Points of agreement and disagreement are listed.

D. Is there sufficient agreement to act? If yes, then the process of theological reflection is finished. If no, then the areas of agreement are set aside and the entire process is repeated. The process ends when there is sufficient agreement to act or when the group finds it impossible to move toward any agreement.

Theological reflection does not automatically resolve conflict situations. In fact, several hurdles might be evident almost immediately. The greatest of these are the different ways participants approach tradition. Some might view Scripture in a fundamentalist fashion. Parish ministers will probably approach it from an historical or critical angle. Some will approach church teaching as if everything is *de fide*. Others might tolerate church teaching only in a highly critical fashion. *Theological reflection succeeds only if there is respect for a plurality of convictions.*

## Questions for Reflection and Discussion

1. Which religious truths do you most easily embrace as you go about living your faith and ministering to others?

2. Do others on the parish pastoral team share your religious priorities?

3. Do the religious priorities of most parishioners match yours? Which of theirs are you most uncomfortable with?

4. Reflect on a conflict situation that was founded on differing religious priorities. How did you deal with it?

# — 17 —

# Adapting to Change

## Biases in Religious Convictions

We saw in the previous chapter that what many people consider important theological truths or official doctrines often are no more than a personal conviction, without objective foundation. These religious convictions, like others such as political convictions, touch deeply-rooted attitudes, even though they may have no historical or theological foundation.

Religion is built upon social structures and dynamics that capture people's allegiances. These include family traditions, inherited attitudes, and even biases. How we view God, ourselves, others, and the world depends upon these dynamics. Parishioners might have strong convictions, even though they have no argument for them; they might defend outmoded practices, even though they no longer observe them. Many people simply do not want their religious convictions challenged or their comfortable practices changed. Their personal security is very much tied up with their religious identity.

Religious formation today is not as cut and dried as it was a generation ago. Nor is contemporary Catholicism as easily identified as its conventional form was a generation ago. In fact, at times there seems to be a smorgasbord of religious notions to choose from as we minister in the contemporary parish. (See Chapter 9, Ministering in a Pluralistic Church.)

A person with a rigid religious identity cannot make these changes easily or comfortably. There will be frequent conflicts with co-workers or the people to whom the person ministers. There will be tension and little thrill in ministry.

## Inevitability of Change

Skill in adapting to change—flexibility that allows us to adapt without undue stress and confusion—is a necessary quality in ministry today. What we devote our ministerial energy to today may radically change in a short period of time; the ground is shifting rapidly under our feet. The structure of the church is changing. The people we minister to are changing. We are changing. How we see our calling is changing.

We live and work in a society experiencing massive cultural change, in a world caught up in global change. Some feel that the very survival of human life is at stake due to lack of environmental responsibility, óverpopulation, and nuclear threats from terrorism-prone countries. We never know where the next armed conflict will be and we do not even know, on a global scale, how to put out these fires of war and genocide—if indeed we ever did. Nor in our own cities do we know how to smother the fires of racial and ethnic hatreds and violence. We feel helpless before such tragedies.

Everything is interconnected and complicated in terms of cause and effect. Current upheavals in economy and job opportunities, in social mores, in family violence—all affect our parishes. What happens on any level of church structure—parish, diocesan, provincial, national, global—affects our ministry and our morale.

## Examples of Change in Church, Religion, and Ministry

Because religion is a human dynamic through which we ritualize and celebrate our relationship with God, some things about it will change occasionally. And if religion changes, of course ministry will too. Almost all features of traditional ministry and liturgical forms have undergone change during the past twenty-five years, some so subtle that they are scarcely noticed, such as in hymn books. Others are major and cause such upheaval; for example, the involvement of the laity in church ministries and in leadership roles.  ˙

Changes in the human dynamics of religion happen more rapidly when shifts in culture are taking place; what influences people's lives will tend to influence their religion as well. The first cultural shift in Christianity happened during the first generation when followers of Jesus began coming from a Gentile culture. Until then, the infant church did not have an identity separate from the Jewish synagogue; Jewish religious traditions had served as their religious context. Gradually radical changes took place: the Greek language for worship, freedom to eat all foods, freedom to associate with other racial, ethnic, and language groups.

A second radical change occurred about a hundred years after Jesus when Christian community leadership of elders and bishops, originally a lay ministry, evolved into a liturgical priesthood.

A third radical change began to take place a couple of centuries later when in the year 313, with the edict of Constantine, Christianity became legal in the Roman Empire. Christians, who had already been influenced by Roman jurisdictional forms, continued to introduce Roman cultural practices into their religion and worship. Imagine these radical changes: genuflections, candles, permanent altars made of stone, permanent temples or churches, vestments, and a new language for worship—Latin.

Each time people experienced a radical shift in their culture and patterns of living, religious changes followed. When the barbarian tribes swept through Europe in the third, fourth, and fifth centuries, the church "Christianized" many of their seasonal pagan traditions; many of which became our popular Christmas customs. About the same time a monastic church evolved, better to serve (and to protect itself from) an "uncivilized" people. The Western church canonized Latin as its official language, while the people preserved their private religious devotions in their evolving vernacular languages. When feudalism swept through medieval Europe, Catholic clergy adopted its forms in the way different levels of clergy related to one another and to the laity.

## Putting Current Changes into Focus

These cultural shifts, with radical consequences on people's religious thinking and practices, occurred repeatedly over the centuries. The most recent one is evident in our own time. An experience of a global society has replaced the conviction that nations can live isolated from one another. Theologians once again reflect upon the mystery of God as found concretely in the cultures of the world. The electronic media and silicon chips become bridges across which people freely move in contact with one another. As part of this cultural shift, the Catholic church is replacing centuries of religious isolation and self-protection with a new openness and ecumenism. The Second Vatican Council is representative of this shift, ushering in another new age of religion, as much in direction and spirit as in documents.

These brief historical notes prompt us to view change as part of the very nature of religious groups. The temptation is to rest secure in the notion that "it was always done this way"; this simply is not true historically. All we can claim is that during our brief lifetime and perhaps during that of our parents, or at most during a certain limited period of history, something was done in a certain way.

Adapting to change calls for humility. We should not think we have arrived at an absolute and final form of religious practice and emphasis. Our religious practices are no more absolute and final than the people who believe, worship, and strive for good moral behavior. (See sections "Religious Identity in Times of Transitions," and "Humility with New Movements and Transitions," in Chapter 11.)

Spiritual stagnation is a likely consequence of being too comfortable with a particular pattern of religious practice. We do not have to make any far-reaching decisions; people do or have done our thinking for us. We may even become complacent.

Adapting to change, however, does not imply that we should race ahead in anticipation of the new. We have a right to enjoy what is truly good in our functioning religious pattern, even while we anticipate a little of what seems to be a new direction or emphasis.

Change is an obvious feature of contemporary culture and, although the pace has slowed down, a fact of the contemporary Catholic church. The ability to adapt to change, therefore, is an important quality of effective parish ministers.

## Questions for Reflection and Discussion

1. What features of Catholicism and parish life have changed most during your lifetime? Did any of these changes affect you emotionally? Which ones seemed to affect family, friends, and parishioners in a rather intense way?

2. What influences of contemporary culture affect your ministry? (technology, art and environment, community structures, etc.)

3. What additional changes in Catholicism or your parish do you hope for? What is influencing the possibility of accelerating your hoped-for changes?

## PART FOUR

# Paying Attention
to Our Spirituality

# — 18 —

# Ministry
# and Creative Spirituality

### Looking to Women and Men of Scripture

Our spirituality is much more fundamental than an accumulation of religious functions, particular patterns of praying, and the pious use of religious objects. It is more a matter of who we are than what we do. It is the most important dimension of our religious identity. We can do holy things and pray holy words, but our spirituality expresses who we really are in relationship with God, our sisters and brothers, and the physical world.

It is often easier to share theological and theoretical insights than to share our personal story, but that is where we find the dynamics of our spirituality. There we find a record of our religious experiences, struggles, and spiritual journeys. Our story tells clearly who we are—if we listen to it. We ministers should know our story well because we speak from it (even if unaware of it) when we share the wonders of faith with those who are traveling their own roads and becoming aware of their own stories.

We can find whole chapters of our own story in the biblical stories of the spiritual wanderings of the women and men of God. A good way to clarify our spirituality is to crawl inside a favorite biblical story and experience how the sandals of a woman or man of God fit us. Doing this also provides general principles of creative spirituality, which we will consider in this chapter.

### Space and Time, the Setting of Mystery

Jacob, son of Isaac, son of Abraham, had a very earthy relationship with God. By hook and crook and a good deal of help from his mother Rebecca, Jacob claimed God's blessings that belonged by tradition to his twin brother, older by just minutes. He found out, though, that these blessings do not fall easily from heaven. Jacob had to flee into exile from his cheated brother Esau.

His journey had just begun when Jacob experienced a fundamental principle of spirituality: All space and time is sacred. He dreamed

> that there was a ladder set up on the earth, the top of it reaching to heaven; and the angels of God were ascending and descending on it. [Jacob dreamed that the Lord was standing over him, blessing him.] "Know that I am with you and will keep you wherever you go, and will bring you back to this land; for I will not leave you until I have done what I have promised you." [Then Jacob awoke and said] "Surely the Lord is in this place—and I did not know it!" And he was afraid and said, "How awesome is this place! This is none other than the house of God, and this is the gate of heaven." So Jacob rose early in the morning, and he took the stone that he had put under his head and set it up for a pillar and poured oil on the top of it. ". . . and this stone, which I have set up for a pillar, shall be God's house. . ." (Genesis 28:11–22).

Every moment of our life and every cubic foot of our living space, playground, office, and ministry locale is a Jacob's ladder. This biblical image describes the mystery dimension of all that is real in life. There is an opening, so to speak, between our daily living dimension—working, praying, and playing—and God's. And, as Jacob experienced, God "stands over" us, blessing us. Everything in our time and space becomes holy. All of our reality becomes God's cosmic temple.

Our memories and celebrations are another essential part of our spirituality. Like Jacob's memorial stone, they mark those ecstatic moments of breakthrough between our dimension and God's. These "memorial stones" are evident in our offices and homes and those of friends. There are special candles, pictures on the wall, photos, prominently placed books and Bible, pieces of driftwood, and even like Jacob's, a stone or two.

Anniversaries of mystery moments past and parties celebrating them today are also memorial stones.

## Struggling with God, a Time of Mystery

Jacob's story—and a model for our spirituality—does not end there in the wilderness. Just like our own, Jacob's story continues and reveals other features of a sound spirituality. Each time he faced a critical transition, he found God there. Sometimes these discoveries, just as the transitions themselves, are a mix of pain and promise of ecstasy. In the story that follows, Jacob, after almost a lifetime, is on his way home to reconcile with Esau, the brother he had cheated years before. Once again he discovers important things about himself. After making sure his family and possessions were safe, Jacob prepared to spend the night on the banks of the river Jabbock.

> . . . and a man wrestled with him until daybreak. When the man saw that he did not prevail against Jacob, he struck him on the hip socket; and Jacob's hip was put out of joint as he wrestled with him. Then he said, "Let me go, for the day is breaking." But Jacob said, "I will not let you go, unless you bless me." So he said to him, "What is your name?" And he said, "Jacob." The man said, "You shall no longer be called Jacob, but Israel, for you have striven with God and with humans, and have prevailed." Then Jacob asked him, "Please tell me your name." But he said, "Why is it that you ask my name?" And there he blessed him. So Jacob called the place Peniel, saying, "For I have seen God face to face, and yet my life is preserved." The sun rose upon him as he passed Penuel, limping because of his hip (Genesis 32:23–32).

This second story of Jacob is especially insightful in regard to spirituality. The person he wrestles with is identified as God. The story, therefore, describes those moments when we feel we are in contention with God, when we feel our way is better than God's way. Jacob does more than give lip service to the all-powerful one. He needs to stop at a critical transition point in his life, put aside the people and things most precious to him, and wrestle with God for a while. This, too, is what we need to do.

Reading this story we can almost hear the grunts and feel the tension as the struggle goes one way and then the other. This God does not give up easily. We all find that out eventually! And this Jacob does not give up easily, either! He finds it hard to submit to the all-powerful and all-wonderful one. He has a thirst to know this God more intimately, a thirst to know God's name.

When the sweat and pain of wrestling with God end, Jacob pants with ecstasy, blessed because he knows he has seen God face to face. There will be other wrestling matches with God, other intimate moments of blessing. But for now, Jacob needs to move on, strengthened to meet tomorrow's challenge: the brother he had sinned against and cheated out of his inheritance: "Looking up, Jacob saw Esau arriving with four hundred men!"

If we are to find mystery inside our own story, we must reflect on it often. It helps to tell our story to a close friend. We have to allow ourselves to laugh and cry as its chapters unroll and fit together. God is there in the jumble of events and in the twists and turns of the plots of our personal story. In a mysterious way, our story becomes God's story. And God's story becomes ours.

## Balance Between Reflection and Action

Another principle of spirituality is balance, primarily between resting in Christ, or contemplation, and the activities of our ministry. One story in Scripture reveals this balance clearly. It takes place in Bethany:

> Now as they went on their way, he entered a certain village, where a woman named Martha welcomed him into her home. She had a sister named Mary, who sat at the Lord's feet and listened to what he was saying. But Martha was distracted by her many tasks; so she came to him and asked, "Lord, do you not care that my sister has left me to do all the work by myself? Tell her then to help me." But the Lord answered her, "Martha, Martha, you are worried and distracted by many things; there is need of only one thing. Mary has chosen the better part, which will not be taken away from her" (Luke 10:38ff).

Unless we rest often at the feet of the Lord as disciples, thirsty for him, drinking in his words, our activity will have no firm foundation, no matter how completely it serves the Lord, his gospel, and the reign of God. We need to combine in ourselves dimensions of both Mary and Martha: a combination of a contemplative disciple and a take-charge worker. Resting in the Lord provides meaning and direction to our active ministry. The balance between this and our work will keep us spiritually, emotionally, and physically healthy. It is achieved best in wholistic living. (See Chapter 19, Ministering with Wholistic Patterns.)

A common affliction of ministry is burnout; the very term is eloquent. There is no longer a Spirit-filled flame giving us the necessary energy to continue our activity, and the burning motive that drives our ministry is obscured. That flame is fueled by a resting in Christ—reflection and prayer—always open to the energy coming from his Spirit.

## Mystery in Hesitation and Fiat

There comes a time when we hear a call, an invitation to do our part in making the presence, power, and love of God present to people at a particular time and place. Our ministry on behalf of the reign of God includes a personal sense of readiness to surrender to the God who invites us to ministry. Our spirituality, therefore, needs a "fiat" dimension to it.

The one who manifested this feature of spirituality perfectly was Mary of Nazareth. When the message came, she did not swoon at the privileged greeting. "'Greetings, favored one! The Lord is with you.' But she was much perplexed by such unexpected words and pondered what sort of greeting this might be" (Luke 1:28ff). We often hear complimentary words similar to these when we are asked to initiate or expand our ministry. We are not being selfish if we hesitate and do some pondering of our own. Mary also seems to have been frightened of what might be coming next because the angel has to reassure her "Do not be afraid, Mary, for you have found favor with God" (Luke 1:30). When the ramifications of God's invitation become evident, Mary still does not blindly leap into a decision. "How can this be . . . ?" Only after being reassured that "nothing will be impossible with God" does Mary firmly surrender: "Here I am, the servant of the Lord; let it be with me according to your word" (Luke 1:38).

We would do well to discern carefully the ramifications of the invitation to ministry that we received. In fact, we cannot honestly say "Here I am . . . . let it be with me according to your word" unless and until we have frankly pondered it and questioned it. Only then will we have a strong and calm "fiat" dimension to our spirituality—and to our ministry.

## Remaining Sensitive to a Different God

A mature spirituality that positively influences our ministry includes a willingness to admit that the God we find at times is not always the God we are looking for. Our pride often determines ahead of time what we want God to be. We want God to be a part of our life on *our* terms.

For a fleeting moment the prophet Elijah experienced a God very different from the one he was expecting. He was shaken from his theological presumptions. While on the run to escape a death threat from Queen Jezebel, the Word of the Lord came to Elijah in his retreat in a cave on Horeb, the mountain of God:

> "Go outside and stand on the mountain before the Lord, for the Lord is about to pass by." Now there was a great wind, so strong that it was splitting mountains and breaking rocks in pieces before the Lord, but the Lord was not in the wind; and after the wind an earthquake, but the Lord was not in the earthquake; and after the earthquake a fire, but the Lord was not in the fire; and after the fire a sound of sheer silence. When Elijah heard it, he wrapped his face in his mantle and went out and stood at the entrance of the cave (1 Kings 19:11–13).

Up to this point Elijah had known the pastoral God of shepherds; the covenanting God of his desert sheik ancestors: Abraham, Isaac, Jacob; the liberating God of Moses; the warrior God of David. His comfortable religious model included a mystery in a burning bush who later gave up the claim to a name; a God of plagues; a God who mapped out the desert path to freedom with a pillar of fire and a cloud of smoke; a God of awful theophanies on holy mountains. Elijah was comfortable with this God who sometimes spoke harshly through his own mouth to both great and little people abandoning their traditional faith, a God who seemed to be competing with another God, Baal.

When God promised to visit Elijah, the prophet naturally expected God to "stay in character," just as we would. For a moment Elijah experiences a different God—a silent, peaceful, gentle God—just passing by!

## Silence and Our Ministry

This image of God identified with "sheer silence" (another translation: "a tiny whispering sound") and "just passing by" has important implications for our spirituality and ministry. A whisper is a very delicate communication that calls for a quiet and peaceful environment or it will not be heard. God's revelation of self has seldom been earth-shattering.

Jesus, the model of every minister, is the prime example of God's quiet whisper. The whisper was heard in the poverty of Bethlehem. Jesus had no need of notoriety or public acclaim. Outside of his own extended family and insignificant hometown of Nazareth, Jesus was not heard of until his Jordan appearance as a mature adult. After that he was popular with people in a small part of a small country but his influence was delicate. His method of teaching was persuasive but gentle: parables and stories. So, too, was his contact with individuals: the woman at the well, the woman taken in adultery, Nicodemus, Mary and Martha, and Zacchaeus. His quiet message did not always sway the masses of people. In fact, there were times when he saw the backs of crowds walking away from him because of what he said. (See John 6:66.)

In the midst of his ministry, Jesus made sure that he kept contact with his God and Father, who comes in "sheer silence," by going off alone to pray. (See Mark 6:46.) This is especially evident when he had important decisions to make and crises to face. (See Luke 6:12, Mark 14:32ff.)

History does not record any world-shaking event or message from Jesus; only the Scriptures of his followers give testimony to his greatness. The most important event—his being raised from the dead—was so delicate that it could be experienced only by committed followers who were left with faith and spirit but no newsworthy proof.

This tiny whisper of God revealing self lies at the heart of our spirituality and ministry. It is necessary, then, to develop an atmosphere that will allow us, and those we minister to, to hear God's revealing whisper for our spiritual growth. Such an atmosphere requires times of silence and tranquility. This will, in turn, require soothing music, pleasant colors, a place of solitude.

The opposite is the case when our environment bombards us with rapid aural and visual stimuli that affect not only our senses but our emotions as well. This kind of environment tempts us to practice a ministry of like kind, thinking that "flash" will be effective. This approach, however, may be like the heavy winds, earthquake, and fire outside Elijah's cave: "the Lord was not in them."⁴ The Lord was in the whispering sound that is so often drowned out in our desperation to attract, distract, and preoccupy.

Ministry is not always, or even usually, calm and quiet. Protests against injustice and racism need to be loud and clear at times. Advocacy efforts get messy. Confrontation, even on a ministry team, can jangle the nerves. This is all the more reason why it is necessary, for the sake of mature spirituality, to find times to rest in the Lord. With a little bit of effort it is possible to find a Sea of Galilee, or a cave on Mount Horeb, and a Mount Tabor for yourself. In that peaceful atmosphere we will hear the "sheer silence" or "tiny whisper" who is our revealing God.

## Questions for Reflection and Discussion

1. Choose a favorite Bible story and find yourself inside it. What does it say about your relationship to God? What other Bible stories reveal other dimensions of your own personal story? How?

2. Describe some of your own "Jacob's ladders" when you experienced your space and time as holy.

3. Describe some "memorial stones" that you use to mark important places and moments in your life.

4. Write your story, paying special attention to the unusual twists and turns of relationships, celebrations, sufferings, etc. When did you feel in contention with God?

5. Is there a good balance in your life? Do you tend to be a "Martha" or a "Mary"? Chart a typical day in your "Bethany." What would Jesus say about the balance revealed?

6. Describe a time when it was important for you to discern carefully the ramifications of new ministry opportunities.

7. Do you have your own "cave on Mt. Horeb"? Think of the environment in which you minister. How does it promote or hinder you from experiencing the revealing whisper of a mystery God?

# Ministering
# with Wholistic Patterns

## Avoiding a Messiah Complex

There is a riveting scene in *Jesus Christ Superstar* when needy women and men crowd in on Jesus in waves, pleading over and over, "Touch me, touch me, Jesus! Heal me, heal me, Jesus!" Finally, Jesus screams in frustration, "Heal yourselves!" Ministry, like many helping professions, tends to consume all our time and energy; it is not unusual that we live and breathe our ministry. There is always more to be done than time and energy allow. We see need all around us, and the more we get in touch with the lives of the people, the more we feel their pain and need. This can lead us to want to "fix" everything in everyone's life.

We may also be tempted to let a few needy people drain our time and energy. When we allow this to happen, they may not always seem to improve. It is not unusual for some parishioners to stake a claim on the attention of each minister who arrives on the scene. It is easy to fall into this trap. It is a very dysfunctional and debilitating match when the "professional" needy person and the minister who emotionally needs to be needed find each other. It is important that when we are drawn to listen and to respond, it is because of someone's true need and not our own.

Feeling called to save the whole parish—and possibly the neighboring parishes as well—is called a messiah complex. Convinced that we can do this is even a greater neurosis. We alone have the answers, we think; we alone have the most effective procedures. And because we are so effective, with crowds of impressed followers, as we see it, we feel empowered to minister alone. We might even glory in the suffering—to the cross!—that our hyperactivity causes. No matter what our gifts, abilities, and desire to help others, we must realize that there is only one Savior, and it is not ourselves.

## Setting Limits

Ministry is a form of work and as such, it is a major source of self-esteem. Besides providing us with necessary economic goods, work fills our need to be productive and so is connected to our personal identity and concept of self. Some of us find our meaning only in our work. We can become addicted to work—workaholics—compelled to work, doing it more and enjoying it less. Some of us have such a need to be needed that we keep people in a situation of dependency —a situation that guarantees even more work. This desire to be needed is sometimes frustrated when people bypass us and insist on "seeing Father" because they have been programmed to find solace and answers only from the clergy. Addiction to work in ministry can be just as unhealthy as it is in other professions and jobs.

Human service professions tend to have a high burnout rate. We become physically, emotionally, and mentally exhausted. We feel depressed and unmotivated to perform activities that once brought us meaning and excitement. The needs of those served always seem to exceed the time, energy, and availability of those serving them.

To prevent this burnout, limits must be set and adhered to. Unions associated with social service agencies wisely set limits and determine hours a service is available, but ministry has no unions and no built-in limits. Theoretically, a minister may be hired for a position for "forty hours" a week, but in reality the job may demand most mornings, afternoons, evenings, and weekends. The same may happen with part-time ministers and volunteers.

Traditionally, Sunday is a day of rest and renewal of body and spirit. A parish, however, is busiest on weekends, when ministers are expected to be present, not only taking part in the worship activities, but meeting other needs that people bring because it is a convenient time for them. Then on Monday they begin their normal work routine, expecting parish personnel to do the same. Doorbells and phones begin ringing.

The parish is never closed; it does not have office hours. The work goes on with liturgies, phone calls, administrative tasks, appointments, meetings, and pastoral visits throughout the day and evening hours. Mealtimes are interrupted. Because parishioners work a variety of shifts, parish ministers need to be available in the evenings and weekends as well as during the day. It is common for parishioners to expect their ministers to be available whenever they want a service. They are not aware that a multitude of other things may be preoccupying us, both parish and personal matters. We therefore have to set limits for ourselves since the parishioners or the pastor probably won't set them. It will help no one if we do not know how to set such limits and stick to them. If we don't, we will pay the consequences with ill health: physical, emotional, and spiritual.

For the sake of *wholeness* in our lives, we need to have a life in which work is but one dimension. It is a very important dimension, to be sure, but just one aspect of a full and whole life.

## Using Time Well

Related to this need to set limits for ourselves is our ability to use time well. "I'm sorry—I don't have time." "Sorry, I'm too busy." "I would like to, but . . ." (completed with any of a litany of activities and commitments). We are familiar with such excuses; if we have not made them ourselves, we have certainly heard them from others when we recruit volunteers for parish committees, ministries, and other activities. It seems that everyone is "busy," or at least they are convinced they are, even if they are retired with no children at home.

Most of us probably consider our time as a scarce and valued resource. And we are wise to view it that way—to a point. Time *is* a valuable resource. Once it is gone, it can never be retrieved and less remains for future use. So, we are wise to be aware of this and use well the time we do have.

An extreme preoccupation with the pressure of time and busyness, however, is not healthy. This is one of the negative aspects of our culture. It is not a gospel value. In fact, insight into the mystery of time and a proper use of it is a Scripture theme. The wisdom of the writer of Ecclesiastes, just after the famous and often quoted "There is a season and a time for every matter under heaven . . ." goes on to reflect on the need to enjoy the fruit of our use of time:

What gain have the workers from their toil? I have seen the business that God has given to everyone to be busy with. God has made everything suitable for its time; moreover God has put a sense of past and future into their minds, yet they cannot find out what God has done from the beginning to the end. I know that there is nothing better for them than to be happy and enjoy themselves as long as they live; moreover, it is God's gift that all should eat and drink and take pleasure in all their toil. I know that whatever God does endures forever; nothing can be added to it, nor anything taken away from it; God has done this, so that all should stand in awe before him. That which is, already has been; that which is to be, already is; and God seeks out what has gone by (3:9–15).

We might also find that our tendency toward busy-ness and our preoccupation with producing ever more and more in a limited amount of time is described in the parable of the rich fool who seems to have killed himself with the drive toward overproduction. The only reward for his labor: "You fool! This very night your life is being demanded of you. And the things you have prepared, whose will they be?" (Luke 12:13–21) We might also reflect on the gospel cautions about the anxiety that accompanies a preoccupation with time's demands and tomorrow's concerns: "So do not worry about tomorrow, for tomorrow will bring worries of its own. Today's trouble is enough" (Matthew 6:25–34).

None of us has one role or responsibility. We minister as spouses and parents, as members of a religious community, as friends, as citizens committed to neighborhood efforts, or even as ministers commissioned for more than one ministry. Even if our ministry is part time, we probably have many responsibilities as students or employees. To live and minister in a wholistic way, it is important to achieve balance as we expend time living out these various roles and the responsibilities that go with them.

The more roles and responsibilities we have, the more urgent it is to balance the way we use time. Each of us has exactly the same amount of time each day, no matter how many roles and responsibilities we have. How we use that time, however, is under our control—with occasional and understandable exceptions.

It is important, therefore, to evaluate how we use this time.

There are practical ways to do this. One is to keep a two-week log of activities in half-hour or hour segments. At the end of this time period, we can determine the percent of our time expended on any specific ministry or other responsibility. This will reveal a pattern of how we use our time. We can then evaluate this. How do we feel about the pattern? How would we like to use this time? This evaluation will give us a sense of our personal priorities.

The next step is time management. We plan to manage our time in such a way that we move from a current pattern to a preferred pattern. All kinds of time management tools are available to lead us through this important step, from fairly simple time management calendars to complex planners complete with how-to seminars, books, and cassettes.

If we get to the point of needing a complex planner, we had better evaluate our ministries and responsibilities. A tightly scheduled, complicated, and detailed daily life is not necessarily the best, healthiest, and most wholistic approach to life. That being said, time management tools can be very helpful if they function as our servant and not our master! They can help us to focus our roles and what is truly important in them. As we become more tuned in to our dreams, priorities, and goals, we can better organize our lives around them. Then, indeed, time becomes our servant, not our taskmaster.

Several good organizers and time-management tools are available, such as the Franklin Day Planner, Day Runner, and At-A-Glance. One that is based on roles and personal goals as a starting point for scheduling is the Seven Habits Organizer, distributed by the Covey Leadership Center in Provo, Utah. This organizer is based on Stephen Covey's books, *The Seven Habits of Highly Effective People, First Things First,* and *Principle-Centered Leadership.*

Among other things, *Seven Habits of Highly Effective People* helps readers to distinguish in their activities what is important from what is urgent. Covey divides activities (life as well as work) into four quadrants: I: Urgent and Important, II: Important but Not Urgent, III: Urgent but Not Important, IV: Not Important and Not Urgent. Covey contends that most people are driven primarily by what is urgent (Quadrants I and III) and therefore they often escape to Quadrant IV activities for some relief. As a result, Quadrant II activities tend to be the most neglected. But, he claims, that is where true leadership lies. We need to train ourselves to give priority to Quadrant II if we wish to be highly effective people in all aspects of our lives.

## Adopting Healthy Patterns

To be healthy—and holy—ministers need balance in their lives. The basics of balance are simple. First, we need to take care of our body through healthy eating habits, adequate sleep, and adequate exercise to provide energy and stamina; otherwise our bodies will not function well. This is basic, yet we probably have poor patterns in at least one of these areas.

Besides taking care of our bodies, we need to nourish our spirits. We do this first of all by cultivating joy and pleasure in our lives. We may be so addicted to work that we find ourselves too tired for simple joys beyond reading a newspaper or watching television. There is more to life than that! There are wonderful friendships to cultivate and support groups that truly nourish us, walks on a beautiful day, gardening to enjoy, and pets and sports to distract us for a while. Cultural opportunities such as concerts and plays nourish our spirit; prayer and reflection integrate our life experiences.

We need to nourish our minds, otherwise we will become dull persons. There are continuing education opportunities in the form of books, workshops, videos, and college courses. We need to learn stress-reducing techniques, anything that we enjoy that helps us put life in better perspective. For one, it might be gardening and walking; for another, it might be various forms of physical exercise; for still another, it might be yoga or centering prayer.

We need adequate leisure time, free from guilt and anxiety, which is necessary for normal emotional development and which provides us with opportunities for play and for other spontaneous activities.

If we are to be _holy_ people, we must be _whole_ people, disciples walking with Jesus on the way to fullness of life—every dimension of life. This challenges us to discover our full potential, not just as ministers, but as human beings. The wonder of wholistic patterns of living is that whatever makes us better human persons, more whole and healthy, also makes us better ministers.

A philosophical axiom makes a good motto for ministers: "You can't give what you don't have." The more we have of fullness of life within ourselves, the more we have to give and share with others. Conversely, the more we give away without replenishing our supply, the less we have to give and the less we want to give. That is when we are most susceptible to discouragement, alienation, unstable living patterns, depression, and burnout.

Being healthy and holy in a wholistic way is enhanced by humor and light-heartedness. Too many people, ministers included, feel that joy and humor are somehow out of place in church matters. A kind of grimness is in order because we are about serious business. The last place anyone needs "grim" is at a parish liturgy or other ministry. These are moments of celebrating the _good_ news, _joyful_ news of the loving presence and power of God among us! An appropriate time for good-hearted humor is at parish meetings. We are about the Lord's mission to be salt and light for the world, to be signs of joy and hope. This is a *bright* assignment, an exciting assignment, not a time for grimness. Many things happen in church ministry that are humorous and we should enjoy those occasions. Even when our work is less than humorous, deliberate humor becomes a marvelous coping mechanism.

Frequently Jesus used the images of a vineyard to describe the reign of God and our ministry. Few of us have firsthand experience of vineyards. The following excerpt from a wine magazine invites us to walk among the vines and learn from them and from the vintner. It can be a source of meditation on the mystery of ministry and the wonder of wholistic living:

> Each week the grower walks the vineyard, looking for signs of disease, or insect attack. A little he tolerates, knowing that it is futile to attempt to eradicate either disease or insect. He weighs the amount of damage the vines can tolerate, the population of the disease or insect, the patterns of growth, the distribution of disease and insect within the vineyard, the forecast weather for the coming days; he uses his knowledge of past years in this vineyard, with these vines, with these pests; with all this in mind he makes a decision to spray not at all, or soon, or to wait. He prefers, in general, to wait, trusting that the vineyard will remain balanced, that weather will cooperate, that pesky insects will be found by predators.
>
> Each day in the vineyard life ends in death, and each day's death brings new life; as the earth revolves around the sun, the eternal wheel turns. This day in May, the grower finishes his tour of inspection, satisfied that all is well, that the season is unfolding as it should. This is a time of promise, the warm sun heating the soil and the vines, lighting the path of growth the vines will take in the coming months, drawing out the growing point, the tip of each vine shoot that pushes upward, always upward toward the sun. And the grower walks home, satisfied" (Mawby, "In the Vineyard—Genesis," p. 9).

## Questions for Reflection and Discussion

1. What elements of a "messiah complex" have afflicted you in the past? Any still present?

2. Have you ever been drawn into a dysfunctional relationship with needy persons?

3. Could you be described as a workaholic? Why? Why not?

4. Describe the balance or lack of balance in your pattern of living and working.

5. Does a time management tool help to keep a proper balance in your ministry? If you do not use one, could it?

6. What do you do on a regular basis that would be called fun?

7. Describe the most humorous thing that happened to you while ministering.

# — 20 —

# Ministry
# and Simplicity

### Finding Our Model in Jesus

What kind of person should an effective lay minister be? We can do no better than model ourselves after the one who is at at the source of ministry and gives it meaning—Jesus of Nazareth. How the gospels picture him in his own ministry provides a clear pattern. What he asked from his friends, apostles, disciples, and people in the crowds clarifies this pattern even more. We will find still more qualities of ministers in the many parables Jesus told about the reign of God, about the loving presence of God among us.

One of the first things we notice about Jesus is his commitment to simplicity. He lived a simple life with few possessions, moving from village to village, a man who could say, "Foxes have holes, and birds of the air have nests; but the Son of Man has nowhere to lay his head" (Matthew 8:20). He found this simplicity in creation and frequently invited his friends and followers to imitate it:

> Look at the birds of the air; they neither sow nor reap nor gather into barns, and yet your heavenly Father feeds them. Are you not of more value than they? And can any of you by worrying add a single hour to your span of life? And why do you worry about clothing? Consider the lilies of the field, how they grow; they neither toil nor spin, yet I tell you, even Solomon in all his glory was not clothed like one of these . . . strive first for the kingdom of God and his righteousness, and all these things will be given to you as well (Matthew 6:25ff).

When we become less and less simple in our lifestyle and begin to complicate it, we experience anxieties. This also happens when we feel we have to do too much or bear more than our share of a particular burden. As we did in an earlier chapter, we should reflect on the scene of Martha and Mary at Bethany and on Jesus' counsel: "Martha, Martha, you are worried and distracted by many things; there is need of only one thing. Mary has chosen the better part, which will not be taken away from her" (Luke 10:38ff).

Jesus counseled simplicity when he sent his apostles out as interns in ministry:

> He called the twelve and began to send them out two by two, and gave them authority over the unclean spirits. He ordered them to take nothing for their journey except a staff; no bread, no bag, no money in their belts; but to wear sandals and not to put on two tunics (Mark 6:7ff).

An old Shaker song, "Simple Gifts," reflects the simplicity the followers of Jesus are called to. It might well serve as a theme for lay ministers:

> 'Tis the gift to be simple,
> 'tis the gift to be free,
> 'tis the gift to come down where we ought to be,
> and when we are in the place just right,
> we'll be in the valley of love and delight.

We may not only complicate our lifestyle; we may also complicate our ministry. The temptation to do this comes easily. The longer we apply ourselves to any particular effort, the more bits and pieces we seem to develop and lay upon those we serve. Jesus urged simplicity in ministering to people. In talking about the leaders and religious ministers of his day, the scribes and Pharisees, Jesus agonizingly says: "They tie up heavy burdens, hard to bear, and lay them on the shoulders of others; but they themselves are unwilling to lift a finger to move them" (Matthew 23:4).

These words should haunt us if we keep adding new and complicated demands on the people we serve. It did not take long in the Christian community for the simplicity championed by Jesus to erode into complexity. In the late second century, Clement of Alexandria (d. circa 215) longed in his _Pedagogue_ for a return to simplicity in ministry.

In war there is need for much equipment, just as self-indulgence claims an abundance. But peace and love, simple and plain blood sisters do not need arms nor abundant supplies. Their nourishment is the Word whose leadership enlightens and educates, from whom we learn poverty and humility and all that goes with love of freedom and humankind and the good.

The history of every religious group or religious movement displays a tendency toward complication. It is part of a predictable cycle: An individual or group enjoys a simple but overwhelming religious experience or insight. Words, actions, and symbols are used to repeat this experience and to share it with others. Sometimes these are new; most often they are old but brimming with new meaning. Soon ritualization occurs from an insistence that all the initiated use the same correct and exact words, actions, and symbols. Early on there is emphasis on a holy literature that guides the leaders and the initiated. Soon there is a need for specialized personnel to hold together and to perpetuate what has quickly become a rather complicated tradition. The personnel experiences its own evolution into specialized groups resulting in further complexity. It is usually at this point that a new "prophet" comes along with a simple but overwhelming religious experience or insight, and the cycle begins all over.

What is true of religious groups and movements is true also of the ministries within them. It seems to be "the nature of the beast" to complicate the simple and to multiply the pieces. Soon we complain about having to hold everything together like a juggler. Burnout of varying intensity is experienced.

We ourselves may be responsible for the growing complication and burnout. When we look at our ministry we can distinguish between all the things we have to do and the attitude we have toward doing them. The two have a powerful effect upon each other. Every ministry involves planning, numerous assigned or volunteered activities, team meetings, staff evaluations, continuing formation opportunities. It involves scheduling and meeting deadlines. Our ministry responsibilities also have to mesh with the ordinary and extraordinary responsibilities associated with our family life and other relationships.

It is not unusual to find that our personal life and ministry have become cluttered. This clutter builds up around us. It can first be the result of handy copy machines, computers, and word processors. It increases with mounds of resource materials we have already purchased and brochures and catalogues that promise to fill still more needs—sometimes needs we have not even felt yet. Even more significant, the clutter is often deep inside us. We allow ourselves to complicate what at first seemed to be a rather neat and contained ministry.

Our attitude toward ministry may also be a cause of some of the clutter and complication in our life. It is not altogether unheard of that a multiplication of activities flows from an unconscious need to justify oneself, one's ministry, one's role in the faith community, or even one's contract.

Striving for the virtue of simplicity does not mean that ministers have to cancel current programs, new insights into ministry, advances in technology, or the commonly used tools of our ministry. People with all these resources can still approach their ministry with simplicity. Why? Because simplicity more than all else is a personal attitude, or approach, toward what we do and how we do it. God's presence and activity in our efforts is very delicate. Complication is an obstacle to the loving presence of God. Simplicity is a bridge to it. Remember the theme of simplicity in the Shaker song: "'Tis the gift to be simple. . . ."

## Questions for Reflection and Discussion

1. Are you overly preoccupied with your ministry responsibilities? How?

2. How do you imitate in your ministry the complications and distractions in society today? How do you witness simplicity?

3. When people have contact with you in ministry, do they find the peace they are looking for, or do they find you full of anxieties because of all you have to do? Explain.

4. Is there someone with whom you are willing to discuss the need to simplify your life and ministry? Do you feel the need to? Why? Why not?

# Ministry
# and Genuineness

### Jesus' Call

Another key gospel quality of lay ministers is genuineness. Jesus looked for this in his disciples and found it most often in the simple rank and file persons, struggling with real life, hungry for bread but just as hungry for filling words. These "little ones" of God, the *anawim*, were sincere, simple, without pretense, and genuine to the core. They listened to his stories, approached him for forgiveness, followed him into the desert, brought the sick to him, and led him triumphantly into Jerusalem. They were the poor in purse and the poor in spirit, the meek, the oppressed, hungry and thirsty for justice. They were the merciful, the sincere, the peacemakers, and the persecuted.

Jesus found this quality of genuineness in the truly "little ones," in children, a quality he recommended for all who would follow him.

> People were bringing little children to him in order that he might touch them; and the disciples spoke sternly to them. But when Jesus saw this, he was indignant and said to them, "Let the little children come to me; do not stop them; for it is to such as these that the kingdom of God belongs. Truly I tell you, whoever does not receive the kingdom of God as a little child will never enter it." And he took them up in his arms, laid his hands on them, and blessed them (Mark 10:13–16).

Some religious ministers among the Pharisees and scribes, who were responsible for leadership and religious fervor in the synagogues, did not have this quality of genuineness. They were afflicted by its opposite: hypocrisy and externalism. Zealous for an exact and formal observance of religious traditions, they prided themselves on being specially chosen, the only true followers of God and the law, a cut above the ordinary people. Jesus condemned the hypocrisy and externalism of these religious leaders time and again. The early church, still in contention with Pharisees and scribes and afflicted by its own hypocrisy and externalism, preserved in their new Scriptures Jesus' counsel about these sins. This is what all parish ministers must be on their guard against. We need to reflect on our motives and patterns of ministry, seeking to remain faithful to the gospel call to be genuine.

In a parable, Jesus epitomized his contempt for this arrogant attitude in some of the Pharisees who merely tolerated or even looked down on the very people they were supposed to lead and minister to.

[Jesus] told this parable to some who trusted in themselves that they were righteous and regarded others with contempt: "Two men went up to the temple to pray, one a Pharisee and the other a tax collector. The Pharisee, standing by himself, was praying thus, 'God, I thank you that I am not like other people: thieves, rogues, adulterers, or even like this tax collector. I fast twice a week; I give a tenth of all my income.' But the tax collector, standing far off, would not even look up to heaven, but was beating his breast and saying, 'God, be merciful to me, a sinner!' I tell you, this man went down to his home justified rather than the other; for all who exalt themselves will be humbled, but all who humble themselves will be exalted" (Luke 18:9–14).

## The Temptation to Hypocrisy

Hypocrisy tempts us ministers to consider ourselves better people than the ordinary parishioners. Worse, when tired and overworked, we might feel mere toleration for the very people to whom we are to dedicate our time and energy. Hypocrisy also tempts us to see ranks in the church community, to act as if there is a division between people and their ministers and leaders, lay or ordained. The exercise of a particular ministry does not make one baptized person better than another. We are all, to use the term of Julian of Norwich, "even Christians."

Jesus condemned externalism, formalism, and artificiality in carrying out good works in our ministry: "Beware of practicing your piety before others in order to be seen by them; for then you have no reward from your Father in heaven" (Matthew 6:1–4). Few of us would go to the lengths that some Pharisees did, exhibiting an extreme religiosity to attract attention, but it is not hard to devise clever substitutes for sounding a trumpet in the parish!

Genuineness helps us avoid extreme religious behaviors in ourselves and warns us about promoting them in others. Throughout his public mission Jesus and his disciples were scolded by the Pharisees for not observing all the little traditions that had become attached like barnacles to their religion. Some of these, such as extreme observance of Sabbath expectations (Matthew 12:2ff, 12:9ff) and the prohibition against contact with sinners and the ritually unclean (Mark 2:15ff), often served as obstacles to the true grasp and appreciation of religion. What had originally been intended to lead to inner perfection resulted in pure externalism. One day Jesus shouted in exasperation: "You hypocrites! Isaiah prophesied rightly about you when he said: 'This people honors me with their lips but their hearts are far from me; in vain do they worship me, teaching human precepts as doctrines'" (Matthew 15:7–9).

If we take a close look, we find in the gospels flesh-and-blood examples of genuineness. Peter, for one, had his faults and Jesus, as we know, had trouble with him—but he was real, genuine; he did not pretend to be what he wasn't. He was human and acknowledged his human condition. This is the kind of person Jesus chose for ministry.

Genuineness calls each person to be what she or he really is. And it is only this real self who can enter into true relationship with Christ and with people. If we are normal we will have faults, but we are not called to lose our uniqueness, to hide our real self and individual personality under a false guise, pretending to be what we are not. To do so will result in a conflict between a true, genuine self and a facade and inevitably impede the effectiveness of our ministry.

Those responsible for ministry formation should never seek to produce stereotypes or cast all in the same mold. Rather, they are to assist in discovering and developing each minister's realness and uniqueness, his or her genuineness.

## Questions for Reflection and Discussion

1. Do you find examples of hypocrisy and externalism within your own personality and ministry? If so, describe them.

2. How could you and co-ministers benefit from a reflection on this gospel quality of genuineness?

3. Is there a feeling of "ranks" within your parish? If so, what are the causes?

# — 22 —

# Ministry
# and Service

**"Here Is My Servant . . ."**

Essential to Jesus' self-identity was his insistence on being at the service of others. He was the man for others who came to serve, not to be served. Avoiding notoriety, he refused any kind of honor or rank among the people, nor did he want his extraordinary gifts and achievements in ministry to become a matter of public curiosity. He respected those he ministered to and those who refused his ministry. He was open even to grave inconvenience if he could help others.

> Many crowds followed him, and he cured all of them and ordered them not to make him known. This was to fulfill what had been spoken through the prophet Isaiah:
> "Here is my servant, whom I have chosen,
> my beloved, with whom my soul is well pleased.
> I will put my Spirit upon him,
> and he will proclaim justice to the Gentiles.
> He will not wrangle or cry aloud,
> nor will anyone hear his voice in the streets. . . .
> And in his name the Gentiles will hope" (Matthew 12:16–21).

Ministry has a way of attracting attention, appreciation, and a period of time in the spotlight. Because our rewards are seldom material, the temptation to seek or at least accept immaterial honors might be harder to resist. Jesus had to face a similar temptation as he began his public ministry. The gospel story of the time he spent in the desert (Matthew 4:1ff and Luke 4:1ff) might very well reflect the temptations of pride, self-satisfaction, and glory-seeking that he faced during his ministry and that we face in ours.

The church of the time of the gospel writers was already a fairly well developed organization with distinct ministries and leadership responsibilities. Some Christians were from the highest levels of local society; others were servants and slaves. These primal communities apparently were bothered by the very temptations to rank and honor and reliance on personal powers that can afflict us. The story of Jesus' temptation in the desert provides a model for our discipleship and ministry. It reminds us that we are never totally in charge of the situations that we minister in; God is. We are called to depend confidently upon God to provide what we and people we minister to need. Any good that we accomplish is due, in the last analysis, to God's grace.

## Jesus' Example

Jesus' counsel and example that disciples and ministers have a true sense of service is a key theme in his good news:

> . . . whoever wishes to become great among you must be your servant, and whoever wishes to be first among you must be slave of all. For the Son of Man came not to be served but to serve, and to give his life a ransom for many (Mark 10:43ff).

> . . . the greatest among you must become like the youngest, and the leader like one who serves. For who is greater, the one who is at the table or the one who serves? Is it not the one at the table? But I am among you as one who serves (Luke 22:26ff).

More effective even than Jesus' words about the self-effacing nature of service is what he did at the Last Supper:

> After he had washed their feet, had put on his robe, and had returned to the table, he said to them, "Do you know what I have done to you? You call me Teacher and Lord—and you are right, for that is what I am. So if I, your Lord and Teacher, have washed your feet, you also ought to wash one another's feet. For I have set you an example, that you also should do as I have done to you. Very truly, I tell you, servants are not greater than their master, nor are messengers greater than the

one who sent them. If you know these things, you are blessed if you do them" (John 13:1ff).

This ritual continues each year at our Mass of the Lord's Supper on Holy Thursday evening. In many parishes the priest celebrant symbolically washes the feet of parish members. This represents his own humility and sense of service in the parish. It would be an effective ritual if all ministers of the parish wash the feet of the parishioners who wish to come forward. In some parishes, the congregation is invited to come forward to have their feet washed and to wash the feet of others. A prolonged and powerfully effective ritual in which parents wash the feet of their children and children their parents' is another possibility.

Ministry of all forms is simply the call to humbly serve the people of God. Important, then, is the attitude we bring to ministry. We may come with an agenda, expecting parishioners and other ministers to fall in line and meet our expectations. This violates the sense of service that lies at the heart of ministry.

Parish ministry often involves tedious or even menial tasks that would not be expected of administrators and other professionals in secular positions. This is especially true of smaller parishes with inadequate staff. There always seems to be furniture to be moved, doors to be unlocked and locked, coffee and refreshments to be prepared, rooms to be cleaned up after meetings, and so on. A sense of service invites us to share these "lowly" tasks, rather than feel we are above them. A sense of service also allows us to feel comfortable with greeting people at the door and serving at table. In a secular corporate setting, to do this is nonsense and a waste of precious time and training. From a servant model of ministry advocated by Jesus, however, it makes sense to pitch in and do our share with the parishioners and other team members.

People's needs often have a way of coming to our attention when it is inconvenient for us. They do not have a crisis or die according to our calendar. A sense of being servant requires flexibility; it shows in our willingness to be at the disposal of others in their time of need, in setting our own priorities aside and graciously providing the ministry needed.

A fine sense of service does not mean that we should be the "flunkie," stuck with all the unpleasant tasks that everyone else is "too busy" or "too important" to do. An important dimension of ministry to is encourage others to assume their own responsibilities, parishioners as well as members of the parish team.

An important part of this sense of service is the gospel counsel to have a healthy respect for all persons and for the differences among them. This is very evident in the ministry of Jesus as he rubbed shoulders with fishers, tax collectors, prostitutes, the leprous, the blind, the handicapped, those possessed by demons, homemakers, government officials, religious leaders. He rejected no one.

Parishioners need to feel recognized and important—and respected. The parish is their spiritual home and family. They want to feel that they are more to us than an envelope number, that they belong to a community and yet are valued as individuals. They should never experience the parish as just another bureaucratic system. Instead, as John Naisbitt suggests in his _Megatrends_, people in this age of high tech are aching for "high touch"; they want to be known and called by name. This justifiable need is a good argument for smaller parishes.

When we first begin to minister in a community, we should take the time to learn the culture, history, traditions, and values of the people we are about to serve. We cannot be aware of this unless we listen to their stories, hopes, dreams, hurts, and complaints. If we do this, we will be on our way toward being a caring and authentic servant of the people.

## Ministers and the Suffering Servant

A sense of service also leads us to put our sufferings associated with ministry into the context of Jesus as the suffering servant. Most lay ministers discover that some Catholic parishioners do not appreciate their ministry and in fact vocally challenge it. Sometimes this challenge comes even from leaders in the church community. These challenges may be accompanied by a form of persecution: gossip, biased assumptions, unfair evaluation, dismissal from a parish ministry. Sometimes this pain, aggravated even by the press, is a consequence of defending minorities' rights, challenging values that threaten gospel values, or vocally resisting unjust systems.

Jesus did not rebel or run away from the cruel and unjust persecutions leveled at him by those who misunderstood his mission or felt threatened by it. As ministers, we are called to walk in his footsteps and to take up our cross and follow him, reflecting on the servant words from Isaiah that Jesus felt comfortable with:

I gave my back to those who struck me,

and my cheeks to those who pulled out the beard;
I did not hide my face from insult and spitting.

The Lord God helps me;
    therefore I have not been disgraced;
therefore I have set my face like flint,
    and I know that I shall not be put to shame;
    he who vindicates me is near.
Who will contend with me?
    Let us stand up together.
Who are my adversaries?
    Let them confront me.
It is the Lord God who helps me;
    who will declare me guilty?
All of them will wear out like a garment;
    the moth will eat them up (Isaiah 50:6ff).

## Questions for Reflection and Discussion

1. Reflect upon your own sense of service in your ministry. How much do you depend upon your own gifts and powers and how much upon God?

2. Are you ever tempted to lord it over those you are called to serve? If so, why?

3. In your experience, do church leaders and ministers tend to be servants?

4. How willing are you to do menial tasks associated directly or indirectly with your ministry?

5. Are you willing to consider yourself one of many parishioners rather than a cut above them?

6. Reflect upon an experience of being misunderstood or unfairly treated. Do the words of Isaiah (50:6ff) help you to put the experience into a more positive gospel context?

# — 23 —

# Ministry
# and Healing

## Jesus' Healing Ministry

All ministry should have a healing dimension; all ministers need a healing touch. Jesus set the example for this as he went about, healing, driving out the demons of physical, emotional, and spiritual brokenness. Through his touch, the power of God struck at the very foundations of evil:

> Jesus went throughout Galilee, teaching in their synagogues and proclaiming the good news of the kingdom and curing every disease and every sickness among the people. So his fame spread throughout all Syria, and they brought to him all the sick, those who were afflicted with various diseases and pains, demoniacs, epileptics, and paralytics, and he cured them (Matthew 4:23ff).

> They had come to hear him and to be healed of their diseases; and those who were troubled with unclean spirits were cured. And all in the crowd were trying to touch him, for power came out from him and healed all of them (Luke 6:18ff).

> Jesus had just then cured many people of diseases, plagues, and evil spirits, and had given sight to many who were blind. And he answered them, "Go tell John what you have seen and heard: the blind receive their sight, the lame walk, the lepers are cleansed, the deaf hear, the dead are raised, the poor have good news brought to them" (Luke 7:21ff).

The followers of Jesus in the early church continued this healing ministry:

> Yet more than ever believers were added to the Lord, great numbers of both men and women, so that they even carried out the sick into the streets, and laid them on cots and mats, in order that Peter's shadow might fall on some of them as he came by. A great number of people would also gather from the towns around Jerusalem, bringing the sick and those tormented by unclean spirits, and they were all cured (Acts 5:14ff).

## Ongoing Brokenness

Brokenness is pervasive in society, afflicting young and old. This brokenness is caused in part by violence of all kinds, which in turn causes more violence. Television brings graphic proof of this into our homes. This brokenness is evident in the family of neighborhoods and nations and in the families of our parishioners.

Parish leaders and ministers of all kinds, as a cross-section of our parishioners, are to some extent wounded and broken themselves. We are the adult children of alcoholics, active or recovering alcoholics, overeaters, and gamblers. We are caretakers instead of caregivers, preoccupied with taking care of the sick, the lame, and the dying. We suffer bouts of depression. We are recovering from injuries suffered in an accident. Some of us are ill with cancer or other diseases. We have had a nervous breakdown. Finally, too many of us ignore our own needs and do not take care of ourselves, slowly harming our general well-being. (See Chapter 19, Ministering with Wholistic Patterns.)

We suffer from an emotional brokenness, the cause of which lies mostly in dysfunctional family experiences. A high percentage of people have not experienced the love, intimacy, guidance, and other nurturing necessary to feel good about themselves, about what they do, and how to form consistently healthy relationships.

Some of us experienced physical or sexual abuse, or grew up in rigid families where love and affection were tightly budgeted or altogether denied. Some of us suffered spiritual abuse from parents or educators who instilled in us an image of an angry, judging "god," which, like so many around us, made us feel even more guilty about ourselves.

Most of the people who participate in our brokenness were not guilty. Our parents, teachers, religious leaders, and various significant others shared with us only what they themselves had and were. And they, too, were broken, each in his or how own way.

The result of all this is an emotional condition popularly called co-dependency. Co-dependent persons never learned how to take care of themselves adequately. They tend to neglect their own needs and wants. Consequently, they do not find peace, security, and happiness within themselves. They become preoccupied with someone else's behavior and needs, with things, with a job or career—or even with a ministry.

New forms of dysfunctional environments cast shadows on people today, causing even greater brokenness. Besides the situations that caused our brokenness a generation ago, our youth today are bombarded by the use of, or at least the news of, mind-altering drugs. They are introduced through movies, television, videos, and music to adult sexual behaviors long before they can cope with them. Some of these stimulants are pornographic or bordering on it. A new form of sexual abuse, therefore, has crept into our culture and family life on almost a daily basis.

Added to these causes of brokenness among our young people is a form of abandonment, a consequence of our family economy. A high percentage of preschoolers are left regularly in some form of day care for several hours and older children become accustomed to a latch-key situation.

Because of all these dysfunctional experiences, a severe condition of emotional brokenness will be evident in our parishes.

## Continuing Jesus' Healing Touch

What practical efforts might we make to add a healing dimension to our ministry, to make present the healing touch of Jesus? The following are some suggestions:

1. First of all, we must be *in touch*. We must make every effort to know the physically and emotionally broken people of all ages who somehow touch our lives. It is important that we spend patient and honest time with them, even though they may not always be pleasant companions or patients.

2. We must deal with our own brokenness, our own story, through growing self-awareness, making use of available therapy and support groups. As we are healed, we will more freely love others in a way that enhances their own emotional and spiritual health.

3. We should tell our own stories, when this is proper, and allow

others to tell theirs, respecting confidentiality. Even young people can be encouraged to come to grips with their wounded selves through general questions such as "What is scary in the life of children your age?" "What makes children like you unhappy . . . happy?"

4. We should relate to groups we minister to as a real functioning or dysfunctioning family. How can the group experience a healthier and happier time together?

5. We are to experience each person as unique . . . and uniquely broken. We are aware of the dysfunctional causes affecting the whole group, but also those things that make each of their stories different.

6. We are to be attentive to each person, letting each know that she or he is special.

7. As much as possible, we should try to be what each person seems to need: affectionate, present, interested in what is happening in their life, supportive, listening, patient, smiling, kind.

8. We should compose prayers that incorporate the kind of brokenness prevalent in the group. We should promote reflection on and pray the Prayer of St. Francis, which speaks so simply and eloquently about the transition from brokenness to healing.

9. We must let people, young and old, know that we are available if they would like to talk, and conduct ourselves in such a way that they would like to confide in us.

10. We should introduce pleasant experiences and good times into our ministries.

11. We should provide information about the effects of dysfunctional patterns in the family. This would be appropriate during special parent sessions related to reconciliation preparation. We should offer resources to support the efforts of families to help them help themselves.

12. We should provide information about support groups that would benefit the family: AA, Al-Anon, Alateen, Adult Children of Alcoholics, CoDa, support groups for child abuse, etc.

13. We should introduce special family events into our parish ministries, such as a "Hugging Day," to support family efforts toward emotional and spiritual health.

Sometimes we have to admit humbly that we cannot do as much as we would like in touching the broken. Even then, if our touch is truly loving, there will be some healing:

Many situations admit of little practical alleviation. Serious illness, physical or mental, may lie beyond anyone's healing. Dreadful ghetto poverty may be something none of us can remove. But genuine care, full of interest and compassion, can sprinkle over the dust a few life-giving drops. We can let people know that we notice their sufferings and their passion, and it moves us to tears. We can share with them our faith. . . . Sometimes this simple sharing . . . gets people through" (Carmody, *Church*, Fall 1994, p. 7).

## Questions for Reflection and Discussion

1. Reflect upon and share some experience of brokenness in your own personal story. To what extent has this brokenness been healed? How?

2. What brokenness have you been protecting in yourself, avoiding possible healing?

3. How does brokenness show itself in those to whom you minister? How have you been relating to this brokenness? How might you in the future?

# — 24 —

# Tapping into God's Dream

### Dreams in Scripture

When Martin Luther King testified—unforgettably—"I have a dream . . ." he was following the pattern of great religious leaders of history: tapping into God's own dream. (See Chapter 18, Ministry and Creative Spirituality.) The Book of Genesis introduces us to this kind of religious experience. God enters Jacob's life by way of a dream, as heaven and Earth are open to each other. In the dream, God repeats to Jacob the promises made to Abraham and Isaac: He would be blessed with a holy land, a great family of countless descendants, and God's own protection.

Jacob did not sit back in his tent and wait for the dream to come true. Like his father, Isaac, and his father's father, Abraham, both of whom had been similarly blessed by God, Jacob actively carved out a life and future for himself and his blood line; things did not just fall into his blessed lap. Only at the end of his life, at rest in the land of Egypt and surrounded by his sons, who became the fathers of great tribes, was Jacob able to see how his own ambitions and efforts, and those of his sons, had accomplished the will and designs of God (Genesis 48:3ff). His own will had coincided with God's; God's dream and his dream had been one.

Jacob's son Joseph also was a dreamer. His dreams pointed to what God willed for him (Genesis 37:5ff): a central place in the future of the patriarch's family. Against all odds, including the drama of being sold into slavery by his own jealous brothers, the dream was realized. Joseph climbed to high positions in Egyptian society and political administration. He was probably well aware of how his own political savvy and ambitions were essential ingredients in his successful career and in his life. His will and God's will had come together. He dreamed God's dream, and God's people were saved for yet another chapter in their sacred story.

## Our Dream
All of us are called to be dreamers, to tap into God's dream for us.

> The dream I have today, my Lord,
> is only a shadow of your dreams for me,
> only a shadow of all that will be,
> if I but follow you ("Only a Shadow," *Glory & Praise I*)

A dream in this sense is not an unconscious jumbled mosaic that occurs during sleep. Rather, it is our most intense desire that develops as years go by. It is the *gradual clarification of what we really want to make of our life*. Our dream pulls together our life's clearest ambition, driving us and motivating us to do and become what is our destiny. Abraham, Isaac, Jacob, and Joseph did not sit back and let life happen to them; they created what happened. They devoted themselves completely to what God had promised them. In this sense they were very ambitious. So were their wives: Sarah, Hagar, Rebekah, Keturah, Rachel, Leah.

This kind of dreaming sounds so human. It is; it happens all the time. We can gain insight into this human but mysterious process by examining a very down-to-earth example. Sitting in front of a fan on a sultry summer day, we might say: "Wouldn't it be nice to have a cottage by the lake?" Years later, at rest in our cottage by the lake, we realize in retrospect how our dream came true. At first, we reflected a lot on what we wanted, possibly to the point of preoccupation. We seemed to be thinking about it all the time, repeatedly reminding our family and friends of our dream. Gradually, what began as a possibility became a probability. Everything seemed to fit together. We made practical plans. We made key decisions. We made the necessary sacrifices. And . . . we have a cottage by the lake!

Obviously, not everyone dreams of owning a cottage by a lake; their dream might be achieving a particular career, or continuing education goals. There are all kinds and levels of dreaming, including the intense desire to find fulfillment in friendship, love, intimacy, peace, justice, or reconciliation. In a *Sojourners* editorial (June 1994), "Can Dreams Come True?" Jim Wallis develops a dream related to recovering the biblical call to justice that will help put our own lives and those of our congregations back in order.

There are dreams associated with directions in our contemporary church and the ministries that serve God's reign. Intense desires related to women's role in ministry, for example, can be a tapping into God's own dream for "all that will be." Like all others, dreams like this will not materialize without action on our part.

## God's Dream and Ours

How can we claim that our dream taps into God's dream for us? If we identify God's dream for us as coinciding with our own most intense desire, might we not be fooling ourselves in order to justify something very selfish? Many of us were formed so thoroughly in the dichotomy between the material and earthy (and therefore tainted with evil) and the spiritual (and therefore wholly good) that we are suspicious of God becoming an intimate part of our reality. This attitude spawned the ancient heresy of Manicheanism: All material things and especially sexuality are evil; only the spiritual is good. Similar convictions still haunt Christians at times. This attitude rejects the revealed truth of the Incarnation. God took flesh and lived among us . . . and has never left.

This dovetailing of our human dream and God's dream matures as we come to faith. Another dream begins to emerge from within us as we come in contact with the limitless dimensions of the Christian story. God's dream, found in revelation, takes on flesh in our own life's challenges as we become more and more committed to a *dream larger than our individual dreams*, the dream dreamed by God's people.

Like our own dreams, this grand dream of God's people does not float in the clouds of abstraction or stay bound in pages of the Bible. It survives and thrives in the very real story of the people who assemble in the local parish. It is there that as baptized people, as a community, we tap into God's big dream. We interpret it in light of our own insights and needs; we make it concrete and contemporary. We share this dream with new parishioners who then experience it and realize it as their own. Yet, even after all these efforts, our dream in the parish will always be just a fraction of the larger dream. There will always be something more to dream. (For an extended treatment of this spiritual phenomenon, see Whitehead, *Community of Faith*, Part III, Fostering Christian Dreams in the Community.)

As parish ministers, we have a special responsibility to tap into God's grand dream. We are very important in making the dream come true, in making it _effective_. We make sure the dream is regularly proclaimed in the many faith formation and prayer opportunities and liturgies that we design, promote, coordinate, or preside at. We do the same at meetings and other assemblies related to our ministry.

Although someone from outside our faith community might be necessary to help us get a particular feature of the dream activated, eventually local parishioners must own the dream and share it among themselves. It will come true only if it excites people's imaginations and desires; otherwise, it will wither and die. It is important, therefore, that we be people of enthusiasm and creativity— and perseverance. There is a need to feel excited for the present and future rather than to feel guilt for the past.

God's dream comes true only if we take the practical, often difficult, steps required. This is why we are involved in responsible activities such as meetings, decision-making processes, budgeting, curriculum development, art and environment, music selection, and community building opportunities.

We have to make sure that one particular aspect of a dream is not overemphasized to the exclusion of all others. If it is, a parish will settle for a narrow, rigid, self-serving, or compulsive dream. This happens when one group begins to control parish plans, or a controlling individual exerts undue influence on the team, or when one mission or ministry is overemphasized to the detriment of others. There has to be a balance in a parish's mission and ministries, and in its influential leaders.

How does a parish go from God's grand revealed dream to its practical realization on the local level? Remember the cottage by the lake? The process is similar. We are always talking about the dream. Every time there is an assembly of parishioners, part of the dream is announced and reflected upon, usually as Scripture is proclaimed. People's attention is kept focused on it. This happens at liturgies, pastoral team meetings, catechumenate sessions, religious education classes, parish council and commission meetings, seasonal celebrations, and community building experiences. We joyfully live the dream ourselves and listen to other people's dream. Dream is added to dream until . . . the grand dream becomes reality.

## Questions for Reflection and Discussion

1. Reflect upon your most intense desire as an individual. Can this be a tapping into God's own dream for you?

2. Identify the most intense dream that your ministry group has. How can this be a tapping into God's dream?

3. With others in your ministry group, compose a creative mission statement, or a dismissal at liturgy or team meetings. It should serve as a practical statement of a current dream regarding some definite aspect of God's bigger dream. It might end with: "Lord, let this dream come true!"

# Selected Readings

Abbott, Walter M., and Joseph Gallagher, eds. *The Documents of Vatican II*. New York: Herder and Herder, Association Press, 1966.

Bausch, William J. *Pilgrim Church: A Popular History of Catholic Christianity*. rev. ed. Mystic, Conn.: Twenty-Third Publications, 1989.

Berger, Peter L. *Rumor of Angels*. Garden City, N.Y.: Doubleday, 1990.

Bergin, Éilís, and Eddie Fitzgerald. *An Enneagram Guide: A Spirituality of Love in Brokenness*. Mystic, Conn.: Twenty-Third Publications, 1993.

Bernier, Paul. *Ministry in the Church: A Historical and Pastoral Approach*. Mystic, Conn.: Twenty-Third Publications, 1992.

Brown, Raymond E. *The Community of the Beloved Disciple: The Life, Loves, and Hates of an Individual Church in New Testament Times*. New York: Paulist Press, 1979.

Brown, Raymond E., and John P. Meier. *Antioch & Rome: New Testament Cradles of Catholic Christianity*. New York: Paulist Press, 1983.

Carr, Anne E. *Transforming Grace: Christian Tradition and Women's Experience*. San Francisco: Harper & Row, 1988.

Cwiekowski, Frederick J. *The Beginnings of the Church*. New York: Paulist Press, 1988.

Chandler, Mary Moisson. *The Pastoral Associate and the Lay Pastor*. Collegeville, Minn.: Liturgical Press, 1986.

Cooke, Bernard. *Ministry to Word and Sacraments: History and Theology*. Philadelphia: Fortress Press, 1976.

Covey, Stephen R. *The Seven Habits of Highly Effective People: Restoring the Character Ethic*. New York: Simon & Schuster, 1989.

Fiorenza, Elisabeth Schüssler. *In Memory of Her: A Feminist Theological Reconstruction of Christian Origins*. New York: Crossroad, 1986.

Haass, Richard N. *The Power to Persuade*. Boston: Houghton Mifflin, 1994.

Hover, Margot. *Caring for Yourself When Caring for Others*. Mystic, Conn.: Twenty-Third Publications, 1993.

Johnson, Elizabeth A. *She Who Is: The Mystery of God in Feminist Theological Discourse*. New York: Crossroad, 1992.

Keating, Charles. *Who We Are Is How We Pray*. Mystic, Conn.: Twenty-

Third Publications, 1987.

Keirsey, David, and Marilyn Bates. *Please Understand Me: Character & Temperament Types.* New York: Prometheus, 1984.

Lawler, Michael G. *A Theology of Ministry.* Kansas City: Sheed & Ward, 1990.

McBrien, Richard P. *Catholicism.* rev. ed. San Francisco: HarperSanFrancisco, 1994.

McBrien, Richard P. *Ministry: A Theological, Pastoral Handbook.* San Francisco: Harper & Row, 1988.

Moloney, Francis J. *Woman First Among the Faithful.* Notre Dame: Ave Maria Press, 1986.

O'Meara, Thomas Franklin. *Theology of Ministry.* New York: Paulist Press, 1983.

Rademacher, William J. *Lay Ministry: A Theological, Spiritual, & Pastoral Handbook.* New York: Crossroad, 1992.

Schillebeeckx, Edward. *The Church with a Human Face: A New and Expanded Theology of Ministry.* New York: Crossroad, 1992.

Treston, Kevin. *Creative Christian Leadership: Skills for More Effective Ministry.* Mystic, Conn.: Twenty-Third Publications, 1995.

Wallace, Ruth A. *They Call Her Pastor: A New Role For Catholic Women.* New York: State University of New York Press, 1992.

Whitehead, James D., and Evelyn Eaton Whitehead. *Community of Faith: Crafting Christian Communities Today.* Mystic, Conn.: Twenty-Third Publications, 1992.

Whitehead, James D., and Evelyn Eaton Whitehead. *Method in Ministry: Theological Reflection and Christian Ministry.* New York: Seabury Press, 1983.

Whitehead, James D., and Evelyn Eaton Whitehead. *Promise of Partnership: A Model for Collaborative Ministry.* San Francisco: HarperSanFrancisco, 1991.

Whitehead, James D., and Evelyn Eaton Whitehead. *The Emerging Laity: Returning Leadership to the Community of Faith.* Garden City, New York: Doubleday, 1986.